DON'T QUIT YET!

DON'T QUIT YET!

How to Handle Co-Worker Friction with
Tenacity, Humor, and Grace

DEBBRA ANNE

Prairie Pond

PUBLISHING, LLC

Prairie Pond
PUBLISHING, LLC

Published by Prairie Pond Publishing, LLC
1868 90th Street, New Richmond, Wisconsin 54017, USA
www.PrairiePondPublishing.com

First Printing, June 2016

Library of Congress Control Number: 2016939797
ISBN 978-0-9968968-2-5
First Edition

This book offers common-sense advice. It is not a substitute for the legal or other professional advice needed in some situations.

Developmental Editor: Beth Wright, Trio Bookworks
Copy Editor: Mindy Keskinen
Cover Designer: Brad Norr, Brad Norr Design
Interior Designer: Ashley Jacobson

Printed and bound in the United States of America

For all who long for a more conscious, mindful work environment

CONTENTS

FOREWORD

I know why you picked up this book. You are sick and tired of co-workers mistreating you, and it needs to stop. You desperately want some peace, but you don't know how to get there. The good news is there is hope, and you don't have to quit your job to find harmony in the office.

As a professional harassment and bullying consultant, I see what happens when bad behavior has gone too far. I am an expert witness for Title IX sexual harassment lawsuits in the workplace. I became a harassment and bullying consultant in part because corporations needed a subject matter expert to provide proper training to employees and management. My job is to consult with clients in developing harassment and bullying policies, investigate complaints, and counsel repeat offenders to improve their conduct and help create a respectful, discrimination-free work environment.

As you can imagine, I've seen my share of bad work behaviors. All employees deserve respect. That's why *Don't Quit Yet!* is so powerful and relevant for today's workplace.

Debbra Anne holds a mirror up to us, challenging us to reflect on our own perceptions and attitudes. She also encourages us to use grace and compassion in dealing with our tough "I don't like you" colleagues. She asks us to examine our own triggers and levels of sensitivity, to use assertive techniques when giving feedback to others, and to always remember to not let their behavior dictate how we will behave.

Don't Quit Yet! tackles topics such as the gray areas around workplace harassment, personal space, co-worker communication, and much more. And it asks whether you want to continue working at your current job. Is your job your passion? Why do you work? If you're unhappy with your current job or employer, why do you stay? Your answers to these questions will help determine how you will handle yourself in the workplace.

The workbook at the end of the book provides exercises to prompt your thinking. For individuals as well as groups, these exercises help to identify sources of co-worker friction and generate ideas for improving workplace culture.

And finally, Debbra Anne offers a wealth of resources, including books and websites. She is dedicated to helping workers soar high with their mindful actions, teamwork, and healthy work relationships.

All employees—including managers and human resources personnel—can reap rewards from this book. With her own tenacity, humor, and grace, Debbra provides us all a great read that can be used to make our work environments enjoyable again.

— Dr. Susan Strauss, RN, EdD,
   Harassment and Bullying Consultant

PREFACE

How many times have you said to yourself something like this? *It's not the job—it's the co-workers I have to deal with that make me want to pull out my hair. I just want to quit my job, stay home in bed, and never go back to that dreadful place. Ever.*

It's tempting to think you're the only one with this thought. But did you know as many as one in three people in the United States are actively looking for a new job at any given time? That's a significant number of workers who have lost their passion, excitement, and enjoyment of life. Why? They let the bad habits and behaviors of their co-workers dictate how they will feel and what kind of day they will have. And a bad day at work almost always trickles down to the non-work hours. You come home and snap at the kids, kick the cat, and yell at the garbage collector because of something that happened at work hours ago. One bad situation avalanches into another and another.

And that might be considered a good outcome. Some workers are so traumatized by their co-workers' poor behavior that violence to others and themselves could result.

Most people think of their own bad habits at the workplace as inconsequential. In part they might be right. Habits like smelling up the office with burnt popcorn, keeping a desk or office that rivals a junkyard, littering the keyboard with greasy crumbs from lunch, or taking long breaks definitely all qualify as bad practices. But what most workers fail to realize is there's a whole host of habits—far more damaging to career success and upward mobility—that are still considered acceptable in many work arenas.

Gossiping, snide comments, bullying, poor email etiquette, being late for work, missing deadlines, invading others' personal space, and functioning from an ego-based attitude are examples of damaging habits. While an isolated incident may not harm your reputation or get you fired, if these habits become routine, they can stop your career dead in its tracks and make it difficult to get hired when a new job presents itself.

Not only do damaging habits and behaviors annoy co-workers, they create tremendous stress for everyone involved. In fact, they're one of the top reasons why workers move elsewhere, even if they like their job otherwise. They hope the new setting will have less drama and bullying, and more respect. But so often that isn't the case. Workers continue to look for that elusive dream job, only to find the same devious co-worker habits showing up time and time again.

Not a laughing matter

In recent years, harassment, bullying, and inappropriate work behaviors have been more readily identified and publicly discussed. But that doesn't mean they have disappeared. Far from it. These problems are on the increase worldwide. More often than not, issues are swept under the rug only to fester and explode later. It's no wonder that in the United States, according to federal government statistics, over seven hundred homicides occur every year as a result of conflicts at the workplace. According to the Workplace Bullying Institute, at least one study shows that people are more likely to have thoughts of suicide after being targeted by workplace bullying. Violence, whether directed toward self or others, may be the result of changes in the brain, which result from "prolonged exposure to bullying and other forms of distress. The brain can become flooded with glucocorticoids, commonly called stress hormones, which reduce capacity for clear, rational thinking."

Some studies show that bullying or psychological violence in the workplace affects almost half of US workers: some are bullied themselves, and others witness it. Arguably, the bulliers themselves may also suffer—their behavior may be a symptom—but they are not included in that figure. The true number affected may never be known because many employees keep quiet, fearing they'll lose their job or be demoted. Isn't it interesting how often the person who is not causing the trouble is the very person who ends up losing their paycheck permanently or being forced to take a pay cut and move to another department? And if that isn't bad enough, many medical problems are also attributable to bullying: high blood pressure, depression, anxiety attacks, insomnia, digestive issues, and even post-traumatic stress disorder.

State and federal laws do protect workers against harassment when it's based on race, ethnicity, religion, or age. But what if it falls outside of these parameters? Unfortunately, the United States has not established any laws against bullying. As of early 2016, there are no plans to address it on the federal level, even though the nation is among the last of the industrialized western democracies to form such a law.

The Equal Employment Opportunity Commission doesn't mandate that companies provide harassment prevention training, but it strongly recommends it. Some states have laws that require training about workplace harassment, but they tend to focus on areas where pocketbooks can be hit the hardest: lawsuits and settlements. This is generally why sensitivity training usually only spells out how employees are to behave so as to not violate state and federal discrimination laws. Sadly, verbal bullying such as name calling, swearing, condescension, and humiliation is completely legal.

It would be admirable if each company went beyond harassment laws and took business ethics into their own hands by creating a set of anti-bullying policies and enforcing them. But many companies avoid addressing situations not strictly covered by law. Why? The reasons include fear of lawsuits (even if they are not substantiated), lack of personnel to monitor and deal with complaints, and perhaps lack of trained managers to handle delicate situations so they don't backfire.

But everything has a cycle. Someday bullying behavior will be more than frowned upon. Laws will be created to deter this type of behavior and quit protecting bullies. More than twenty states have already introduced anti-bullying legislation known as the Healthy Workplace Bill, but as of this writing, no bills have been formally passed. Still, as you might recall, the United States took decades to criminalize domestic violence and child abuse—so maybe someday bullying at the workplace may also be seen as a punishable crime.

What's in it for me?

I'm not here to tell you all your co-worker issues will magically go away if you simply wear blinders and tape a smile on your face. But this book will show you how to navigate co-worker friction, the subtle forms of bullying, and annoying behaviors. You'll learn to reset your inner dialogue so it doesn't continue to sabotage your work happiness and success.

If you're dealing with a co-worker's poor habits, you'll learn how to take action when appropriate, and you'll learn how to judge when it's wiser to turn off your mind chatter and disconnect from the problem.

If you're the one with a bad habit, you'll learn first to recognize that your behavior is nonproductive, then to create new actions that are more functional and steer you toward more conscientious habits.

You'll discover that listening to your own intuition and guidance will provide a wellspring of authentic knowingness that is instrumental in propelling you through your day-to-day heavy load. In turn, you'll naturally be steered toward more ethical behavior choices, and you'll look to others to follow suit because your own conscious work behaviors have grown and changed forever. No longer will it be acceptable to just live with bullying and poor behavior choices from co-workers.

The goal is simple: to get along with co-workers, and to work in a harmonious manner that offers respect, compassion, consideration, and increased productivity.

What qualifies me to write this book? While I have a BA in journalism, I don't have a doctoral degree in psychology, nor am I a harassment consultant. But I've lived in the trenches of corporate America for over twenty-five years as a purchaser, planner, and account manager for large and small manufacturing companies. I've witnessed many appalling situations that make me shake my head and wonder why good workers are forced to quit, change departments, or invent a coping mechanism just so they can earn a living.

I am simply a person who wants businesses to awaken to the notion that we are doing our workers a disservice by allowing poor behavior to continue in the workplace, and we need to up the ante by learning to give respect to others. It's not okay to keep on doing what we've been doing.

So let's look at how you can iron out those co-worker conflicts. Don't quit yet!

INTRODUCTION

THAT'S IT! I QUIT.

That was the thought I had, rational or not, after being annoyed with my co-workers for the millionth time.

Strike that. For the *last* time.

Don't *walk* out the door, I told myself. *Run* as fast as you can somewhere—anywhere—as long as it wasn't where I was standing right now. My co-workers had almost pushed me over the edge, and I wanted out. No amount of talking through the political drama, no pay raise, no office-space shuffle would suffice anymore.

Enough was enough. I was on to a better job where well-behaved employees would work in peace and harmony.

I have to admit, deciding to quit my job that day was one of the most freeing moments of my life. I hadn't actually given my notice yet, but I took a break and walked out into the sunshine with a smile on my face. There was a certain peacefulness that followed, as if a dark cloud had been cleared away and I was finally free to start my life over as I wished.

Was it asking too much to work with adults who wanted to interact with the human population in a positive, team-like manner? And what gave my co-workers the right to belittle people, whispering behind their backs but smiling to their faces? Work wasn't supposed to crush the human spirit. It was supposed to be a place where people enjoyed their jobs and learned skills useful to the world. And if they didn't find a job they were passionate about, at least they should enjoy the people they worked alongside.

I decided it was not acceptable to allow co-workers to treat each other poorly. Sure, we live in a free country with free speech, but that's no excuse to indulge in unethical conduct. With freedom comes an unwritten precept of responsibility.

Yes, occasional flare-ups of annoying behavior can probably be dealt with, but if done on a continual basis, they soon lead to being perceived as a bully. And what happens when the boss or the human resources manager turn their heads from a sticky situation when dealing with a difficult co-worker? It leaves victims in a precarious position, often feeling beaten down and without good options.

Worse yet, workers who are unable to vacate a job because of a flat economy or lack of employment alternatives could decide to "quit and stay." I now understood the deep emotional turmoil that plays in the minds of trapped workers.

In this era of personal branding, I wondered why someone would jeopardize their reputation. Many people take time to dress nicely as part of their brand image. But doesn't brand identity also include writing professional emails, showing up on time to work, not facilitating gossip, and speaking kindly of others?

Frustration had definitely set in. Perhaps I was looking for a work environment that didn't exist—and never would.

I suspected bad work behaviors boiled down to one thing: fear. Unconscious and conscious fear of rejection, with hints of inflated egos; fear of the unknown; and fear of finding passion and living life to the fullest.

I realized that bad behavior is contagious. When one person pulls down the invisible code-of-conduct flag with no repercussions, it gives others permission to violate as well.

I decided to talk to a friend who had recently changed jobs. I anticipated—relished actually—what she would say about her experiences. How the new work environment was a vast improvement. Maybe she'd tell me it was a place where employees arrived early just because they enjoyed the company of their co-workers. I started dreaming of having my own love affair with my career, hobnobbing with colleagues who were passionate about work, life, and love, and the great strides we'd make, not only as a workplace but in personal fulfillment. Something akin to the "googliness" that I imagine Google employees must feel as they thrive in an open, sharing environment.

But after dinner with my friend, that's when the salty, gritty taste returned to my mouth. I came to the conclusion that every place of work has its share of annoying behaviors and drama. They weren't just tainting *my* office—drama and bad behaviors were everywhere.

But I also began to see something else: not every irritating person was annoying all the time. It might be easy to get along with a co-worker most of the time, but now and then some annoying habits bubble to the surface, occasionally erupting into full-blown jerkhood. But, I thought, maybe that so-called jerk was struggling with personal or family issues: maybe that was the source of all that molten lava. It's no wonder we have mixed feelings about these people.

Needless to say, my determination to quit my job began to wane. Then panic set in.

Where could I go to get away from these people?

The resounding answer came from within. *Nowhere*, that quiet, knowing voice answered. *You have to live with them. Just as they have to live with you.*

Then an idea started to solidify. What if there was a way to deal with difficult situations that fostered the work relationship rather than tearing it down? A way to create coping mechanisms that allow employees to feel happier in their environment, regardless of the chaos going on around them? I decided it was worth investigating. What did I have to lose, other than the job I was on the verge of quitting anyway?

Suddenly, I felt a lightness in my step, as if a great weight had been lifted from my body, making way for a stream of higher consciousness. I sensed that my mission had been revealed in my hour of darkness. Solving this problem could indeed heal "broken" workers. But it could also heal my own dark night of soul as I struggled to find fulfilling work, enjoy my journey with fellow co-workers, and make it all a meaningful experience.

In that moment, I decided I wouldn't quit yet. Instead, I'd set out to find my truth and understand how we can work together, or at least get along, in the workplace.

I wanted to know how to deal with the pressures that everyone experiences and do it in a way that is life-changing, in a positive way, rather than quitting my job and discovering the same problem in a new setting, again and again. I wanted to know how to stay out of the human resources manager's office and feel empowered to make changes myself, within myself. I wanted to experience an internal attitude adjustment that would resolve a problem in progress, or perhaps dissolve it before it even had a chance to crystalize and turn ugly.

HR and management, this is for you

If you are a human resources professional or a manager picking up this book, I want you to find guidance. When frustrated employees knock on your door crying, fed-up, or ready to walk out the door, you can offer advice on handling a problem between co-workers. I'm not talking about legal advice—you should seek legal counsel if a situation has crossed that line. I'm talking about advice that helps an employee respond to behaviors that are obnoxious and create friction to the point of unproductivity.

With this book, you'll have examples and stories to share with an employee about how others solved a work dilemma or worked through a problem so they were able to get back to a productive state.

You'll have tools, such as the ideas discussed throughout the chapters and the workbook at the back of the book, to help you plan a workshop that will improve employees' interpersonal skills in a workplace context.

You'll also be able to help employees appreciate our individual uniqueness and see that treating each other poorly goes against the moral, virtuous, and noble laws of the universe. You will play an important role in keeping employees free from the web of fear, conflict, and even legal situations.

Employees, you're not alone

If you are an employee in the midst of chaos, I want you to recognize you're not the only one who's had bad experiences with co-workers.

You're not alone in the least.

But running from the problem only makes it better for a while, and after the honeymoon phase, sooner or later you'll find that a similar problem has cropped up at your new place of employment.

The only way to resolve the problem is to look inside yourself and delicately examine your views, attitudes, and ways of handling conflict. No one else can solve your problems but you.

This book helps you find that well of courage to tackle the hard problems head on and change your thought process so conflicts roll off your back as easily as paper through a printer. You might even realize courage was always there, under a mountain of fear. It just needed a little help in finding the right way to express itself.

What if I discover I'm the one with the behavior problem?

Congratulations! Pat yourself on the back. Really, I mean it!

Most people never own up to their bad behavior. They prefer to bury their own actions in the sand while excessively examining others' wrongdoings. Even after years and years of being in the same fearful and sad place, they continue to pretend nothing they do is wrong, inconsiderate, or close to bullying. They walk all over quiet-spoken employees and allow poor behavior to run rampant.

The fact you have identified your behavior as unproductive is huge progress. Now you can go to work setting new goals to include patience, kindness, and consideration, and ultimately moving your career forward following a higher code of ethics. Forming new habits takes patience, but don't give up. Your whole life could change from this one important decision.

You have a choice

In the end, you can make the decision to keep doing what you've been doing—walking away from an incident feeling as if you're powerless, depressed, and stuck. Or you can take responsibility for your work contentment and change your situation for the better.

\ | /

THERE'S A CERTAIN

EXHILARATION

WHEN A GOSSIP-LOVER

REVEALS A TANTALIZING

SECRET TO A PEER.

/ | \

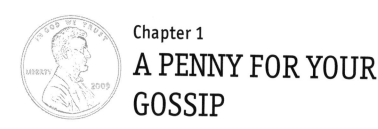

Chapter 1
A PENNY FOR YOUR GOSSIP

H AVE YOU EVER SEEN TWO CO-WORKERS WHISPERING IN the corner and then glance your way? A cold shiver runs down your body as you get the distinct feeling the conversation is about you and your private affairs. Do you sit there and try to ignore it, or do you go and stand up for yourself? Unfortunately, we've all been the target of distasteful gossip at one point or another. It doesn't matter if it's true or not, it causes stress, diminishes teamwork, increases absenteeism and turnover, and stops us from doing the work we were hired to do. That's why this conflict is one of the most common, and offensive, on the list.

Who's talking about me?

Gossip has probably been around since the dawn of the cave people. Can you imagine what that sounded like? *Ooog, Wilma, you see Lucy by rock? She stand there, do nothing when everyone cook mammoth meat. She wear ugly T-Rex boots and Saber-tooth tiger dress, smell like wet mastodon.* Snicker. Snort.

While that may be humorous, the fact that gossip has been around that long isn't funny at all. It wasn't until later that humans put an actual label on it. Around the 1400s in England, the word "gossiper" gradually transformed to mean a familiar acquaintance, especially a woman friend who was invited to witness a birth. In the 1500s, the meaning was extended: it became a non-derogatory word for a person, generally a woman, who talked about others with friends. Later, around the 1800s, the word transformed yet again, referring to one who engages in groundless rumors. That definition has stuck with us, having moved far from its earlier cozy connotations.

Today, to call someone a gossiper in the workplace is undeniably derogatory. A person with this habit can cause many problems—some severe and even illegal. At its best, gossip is simply information passed on to another. At its worst, it can be seen as a form of attack: it can ostracize workers, build power in the gossip initiator that wouldn't have otherwise been there, and punish those who step out of the norm.

We in the United States have become a very gossipy culture. You don't have to go far to find that our society loves gossip, blessing it as more than just an acceptable practice—it's become the fabric of our news. With the growth of the internet, celebrity gossip magazines such as the *National Enquirer* and "news" shows like *TMZ*, many have made millions from passing on updates on the activity and misery of others. Hollywood definitely has a love-hate relationship with gossiping: celebrities love the attention and free publicity, but don't want their privacy disturbed or personal information used against them. The general public certainly has become numb to this method of news dissipation and have embraced it as the norm.

There's a certain exhilaration when a gossip-lover reveals a secret to a peer. The latest gossip can enhance social status: one is seen as an "authority" as others come to them for news. The chain can then be perpetuated, as the receiver now has the choice to become the gossiper.

And that tidbit of gossip? It can become diluted, changed, and even heightened in details depending on the circumstances and how the message was received. Not exactly reliable information.

Why . . . why . . . why?

What makes people want to gossip? Why is it so fascinating to participate in this time-wasting activity?

The short answer is that people want to feel connected to others and find common ground. They want a bond with someone who is on their side. The old saying "Misery loves company" rings true, and with gossip it is perpetuated. But what the gossiper may not realize is that this activity can be very damaging.

Gossip can make people paranoid as it spreads through the office like wildfire. Everyone starts to wonder what others are saying about them behind their backs. It also wastes the time of everyone in earshot—not only do the gossipers stop working to spread their rumors, but everyone else tends to be less productive when straining to listen in or wondering if the talk is about them. Is an important detail of work drama being leaked? Or is it of a more personal nature? Maybe someone is on the "office troublemaker" list, and that unfortunate soul is me.

In many settings, gossip seems to be a fact of workplace life. Perhaps HR staff, managers, and bosses even unconsciously condone it to do the secret dirty work for them, such as breaking undesirable news, creating an air of fear so behavior is kept in check, and clueing in new employees of expected norms so boundaries are not overstepped. Allowing gossip reminds workers of other's misfortunes so we're more likely to avoid the same situations. Gossiping, in these instances, fills the cracks that aren't directly communicated, which can be a useful tool in keeping workers from wandering too far outside of the rules. Imagine if HR or management had to tell each employee each little detail of job behavior that they considered wrong or right.

The Good Kind of Gossip

Positive gossip, about people doing something well, had "self-improvement value" for participants (in a study from the University of Groningen in the Netherlands) as an example of how they themselves could do better. Negative gossip did indeed make people feel better about themselves, but it also made them more fearful that they might be gossiped about, too. After all, hearing negative gossip meant they were in an environment where people gossip negatively about each other. They could be next.

—Julie Beck, "Have You Heard? Gossip Is Actually Good and Useful"

Still, gossip can be damaging on a deeper level. More often than not, it is hurtful, flippant, and filled with subjective opinion. And if that's not enough, the act of gossiping wastes time, creates uneasiness, increases absenteeism, and ostracizes. Ultimately, it snakes its way into productivity, eating away at the bottom line, and manifesting bad blood between team members.

It wasn't long ago that an employee of the White House gossiped on her Twitter account about one of the president's young children. It was in poor taste, and her employer quickly found out. Needless to say, she was promptly fired. A note to remember—what goes around comes around, sometimes in the swiftest fashion.

Early in my career, I thought gossiping was an acceptable method of business communication. I quickly found out that it can backfire. I had passed a confidential piece of information to a friend. Somehow the fact that I had leaked it got back to my boss.

Needless to say, he was not happy, and he discussed it with me—lucky for me, privately. With that faux pas, I sacrificed being ethical, I betrayed my boss's trust, and I found myself in the "naughty box"—all so I could have a brief moment of illusory power. Not only did I learn who my friends were, but I learned a valuable lesson in obeying the law of silence. Not exactly a shining moment. It has since been a habit I have tried to wipe out of my workplace etiquette.

I made a personal rule that if I can't say something nice, kind, or true—out loud—then it probably should not be said at all. Besides, it's karma I can definitely do without.

Gossiping can be a hard habit to completely erase, especially when a superior is involved. An instance came up that tested my resolve. As I was walking back to my office from lunch one day, my manager happened to walk in with me. Maybe out of nervousness or wanting to be seen as being friendly, she asked what the latest gossip was. Can you say *awkward*? If I told her anything, it would violate my code of ethics. If I didn't, I could be seen as a snob, or worse yet, as someone who wasn't viewed as a team player. I don't think she realized the predicament she had placed me in.

Thinking on my feet, I decided to tell her a half-truth—simply that I didn't know any gossip. That way she wouldn't view me as a source for that type of information, and I wouldn't have to explain my code of ethics, which could have caused embarrassment for both of us. She never asked me that question again.

If gossiping is ever going to be wiped out, or at least limited, expectations need to be communicated from top-level management. If there is no formal policy, then at least providing a good example goes a long way.

Stopping the gossip cycle

The easiest and most direct way to avoid engaging in gossip is to tell a gossiper you're busy, and unless it's something that is important or vital to business, you need to concentrate on the task at hand. You can also say, "I don't like to talk about other people, because then I set myself up to be talked about."

Another way to manage it is to recognize that gossiping is some people's way of dealing with fear. Take the high road and ignore it. It's not that you're better than the gossipers are, but they are doing the best they can in the world they live in. If they were more conscious of their poor behavior, they would know it hurts people.

Your internal ethics

You might be surprised to find that the reason gossip in the workplace bothers you has more to do with your internal issues than with the gossip itself.

Before your ego has a chance to draw up a list of arguments, let me explain.

A friend once asked me what it was about gossiping that I found so offensive. Isn't it obvious? I scoffed. It's unkind and unproductive. But if the gossiping isn't about me, she asked, why do I care? Even if it *is* about me, why do I care about someone else's opinion?

The digging persisted. My ego was getting a black eye and didn't like it one bit.

Then she asked the million-dollar question: Why do I care if gossipers aren't productive and take longer to get their work done?

It was then the true issue was brought to light. I reflected and realized the problem. I work hard during regular business hours so I can leave on time to attend to my family, but the gossiper often had to stay late to finish their work. And I was afraid the boss would think they were a better employee for staying late. It really had nothing to do with gossiping.

What? This problem actually boiled down to my own insecurity about my status at work? My fear?

I realized the only way to shake off this feeling of victimization was to acknowledge it, quit allowing my ego to link it to my own work behavior, and then of course release those crippling thoughts so I could get back to a more productive state.

Ways to quit gossiping

Become conscious of what you talk about with others. Create conversation rules for yourself and follow them, and don't allow yourself to get sucked into gossip. You may find you have a lot less to say because it doesn't meet the standards of being kind, true, and necessary. Stick to facts, but be careful, because opinions can feel like facts—that's a sign ego is involved. You may lose some friends as a result of your newfound ethical habit. And you may realize in short order they never really were your friends in the first place.

In the end, I think Socrates was right: "Strong minds discuss ideas, average minds discuss events, weak minds discuss people." Interesting words to ponder.

THREE TIPS FOR KICKING THE GOSSIP HABIT

1. If someone begins to engage in gossip, tell them you're busy and walk away.

2. Make a rule for yourself: if you can't say something out loud that is appropriate, kind, and true, then don't say it at all.

3. Realize that the reason gossiping bothers you may be more about your internal issues than about the gossiper. Drill down and figure out why. Then let it go.

\ | /

A KNOW-IT-ALL CAN

BE THAT BUZZKILL

THAT SEEPS INTO YOUR

DAY AND FLAVORS IT

WITH LEMONS.

/ | \

Chapter 2

EXCUSE ME, YOUR BIG EGO IS STEPPING ON MINE

KNOW-IT-ALLS CAN BE SOME OF THE MOST INTERESTING, and obnoxious, characters we work with. Suspects come from all walks of life and can thrive in any position. Perhaps it's someone who's worked at the company for a long time, or it can even be the boss. While it might be evident the person is smart, there's nothing more off-putting than people who think they have all the answers—sometimes before the questions are even asked.

I can't help but pick on the stereotypical IT worker. Now, before the whole computer team comes over and threatens to take my system off the grid, I want you to know I have a deep respect for IT workers. Some of my family members work in the IT field, so I know how stressful and demanding it can be.

There is no doubt that some of the smartest people in the world make magic happen by punching a few keys, ending our computer woes in a New York minute. But it's the attitude of superiority that sometimes accompanies the role—the dreaded God complex—that can be a serious obstacle to good work relationships. That moment of success disappears faster than free bagels in the lunchroom. A know-it-all can be that buzzkill that seeps into your day and flavors it with lemons.

You might be wondering, why are know-it-alls a workplace problem? Don't they provide valuable information to co-workers and management, thus keeping productivity going? Well, the answer is yes. And no.

Employees who have their fingers on the company's pulse are great resources and deserve a pat on the back for their loyalty and ability to go the extra mile. Some may be perfectionists who truly care about the well-being of the overall business, but they take it so personally that they actually hinder progress. They may wonder why others don't care as much as they do or don't feel the need to work long hours. They are so caught up in their own agendas that they fail to look at the big picture.

Again, why would this be bad? In a meeting, a person who thinks they already know all sides of the story is less likely to actually listen. That person might speak compellingly, but new ideas tend to be tuned out. Less vocal individuals are overpowered, and creativity is stifled. If this constant heavy-handed attitude is accepted, there is no growth—for the company or the individual.

Creativity is a word that all companies must live by. . . and die by. In this world of fast-paced politics, finances, and inventions, creativity is often the only asset a company can rely on to get it through to the next day. Without it, failure is certain. Every day must be won with new ideas, new ways to be productive, new systems to make work easier and less costly. If a know-it-all has the reins, the lights might soon go out in the shop.

Perhaps you've been in a meeting when the know-it-all boss reveals to the management team a grand plan to reorganize the office area. The boss pulls out a sketchbook from the bottom drawer and says, this is the way it will be done. No comments are solicited or research offered up; the declaration that things are changing is simply stated without option. While the boss has the right to decree change, it is the attitude that loses the war. Common courtesy and asking for others' creative insights could make all the difference in gaining goodwill and true cooperation.

I'll never forget the time a co-worker decided he knew all the facts about a given project and proceeded to skip a meeting where other information would be provided. He not only ended up doing the project incorrectly, but he cost the company money because a product was delayed in release to market.

The best defense

When working with a know-it-all, do your research diligently ahead of time before talking to them about a business matter. Don't waste their time by flinging out unconsidered opinions, because they'll never make the grade with the know-it-all anyway. Instead, first investigate thoroughly, examine facts, and scrutinize the options to uncover the best solution. To a know-it-all, if you can show your string of research and how you arrived at your solution, it's like whipped cream on that mocha. You are much more apt to get the respect you deserve with a little forethought.

Listen carefully to a know-it-all. Hear them out—they probably have useful information. But don't let them railroad you. It's not a time to be shy. Be assertive, not aggressive. It is a fine line that will lead you to success.

If you can't seem to coexist with a know-it-all, in the end it may be best to agree to disagree and walk away to fight the fight another day. Especially if leaving the company isn't an option, the best strategy may be to keep your distance, so your two egos can't get entangled.

The Ego's Favorite Thing

Complaining is one of the ego's favorite strategies for strengthening itself. Every complaint is a little story the mind makes up that you completely believe in. Whether you complain aloud or only in thought makes no difference. When you are in the grip of such an ego, complaining, especially about other people, is habitual and, of course, unconscious, which means you don't know what you are doing.

— Eckhart Tolle, *A New Earth: Awakening to Your Life's Purpose*

Dig a little deeper

Ask yourself why the know-it-all's behavior bothers you. Here, another important life lesson presents itself.

If it were possible to focus a microscope on your own ego, you'd find it is likely the culprit. It can't stand someone being smarter and cleverer. The ego believes that if someone is "more," then it has to be "less." Ego loves to rank people with neat titles such as "idiot," or some other offensive description, to make it feel better. It doesn't understand, nor does it care, that people are connected, and each person possesses wisdom that is an asset for the whole. The good news is the moment you shine that light on your ego, you have the opportunity to see it for what it is and move past it.

Remember, when you're dealing with ego, it doesn't want to know the truth. It only wants you to feel good. When a know-it-all tramples all over your truth, the only way to continue in good spirit is stop for a moment. Forget that your ego just got kicked down a notch. Acknowledge your feelings: resentment, anxiety, disappointment, fear. Ask yourself if those feelings are truly warranted. You'd be surprised how many lies we tell ourselves to feel better. Decide what is right, fair, and honorable given the situation. At this point, ego disappears and then you know you're working from the heart. By actively listening, the real truth is revealed. You might realize the know-it-all is actually right— or you might find the fortitude to walk away knowing you simply have a difference of opinion.

When in a conflict, co-workers often contradict one another. They hear only the weaknesses of a co-worker's argument and not the strengths. But if active listening occurs, both parties can find common ground and are more likely to cooperate with each other.

"Most of us are not good listeners," says Dr. Susan Strauss, a harassment and bullying consultant. "While the other person is talking, we are already thinking of a retort, thereby not focusing in on their message. When I conduct communication skills training and engage participants in active listening, they are amazed at what a difference it makes when they experience the other person *really* listening to them—they feel honored by the real interest the listener portrays in them and their message."

Are You Listening?

Active listening is a way of listening and responding to another person that improves mutual understanding. Often when people talk to each other, they don't listen attentively. They are often distracted, half listening, half thinking about something else. When people are engaged in a conflict, they are often busy formulating a response to what is being said. They assume that they have heard what their opponent is saying many times before, so rather than paying attention, they focus on how they can respond to win the argument.

—"Active Listening," Conflict Research Consortium, University of Colorado

If you're still wondering why a know-it-all pushes your buttons, perhaps you might look for ways to become stronger yourself. Without necessarily being confrontational, become a greater advocate for your own views and knowledge.

Emphasize the positive, rather than the negative, by listening to the small voice inside and looking for the good, or the lesson, in each situation. Finally, build a more stringent internal thought system, one that lasers in on ego-based behaviors and redirects your focus to what really matters—the good work you are there to perform.

Practicing mindfulness

Mindfulness training has Buddhist roots and is becoming recognized in the Western business world as a way of dealing with work tensions and thwarting ego-based behavior. It is the practice of purposefully paying attention, and it's been found to lower stress and depression, increase focus, and foster co-worker camaraderie.

In recent decades, Jon Kabat-Zinn has renovated this ancient practice and brought it into the mainstream. A teacher of mindfulness meditation and author of many books on the subject, he also founded the Mindfulness-Based Stress Reduction program at the University of Massachusetts Medical Center. Wildmind, an organization that promotes Buddhist meditation, includes this description in its introductory materials:

> Mindfulness is an emotionally non-reactive state. We don't judge that this experience is good and that one is bad. Or if we do make those judgments we simply notice them and let go of them. We don't get upset because we're experiencing something we don't want to be experiencing or because we're not experiencing what we would rather be experiencing. We simply accept whatever arises. We observe it mindfully. We notice it arising, passing through us, and ceasing to exist.

Practicing mindfulness allows a person to see a co-worker's rude actions but not react to them or judge them as good or bad. The mindful person allows the emotion to pass and goes back to focusing on the work at hand.

In the past, many company leaders have thought this practice to be esoteric and perhaps crossing the line into spiritual territory, but it is becoming more and more accepted in the workplace.

In her article "Workplace Mindfulness Can Aid Focus, Employee Bonds," Traci Pedersen reports that "organizations such as Google, Aetna, Mayo Clinic, and the United States Marine Corps use mindfulness training to improve workplace functioning." The growth in this field has much potential as companies strive to find fresh ways to cultivate work relationships and increase productivity.

The universe is a mirror

A know-it-all I worked with was notoriously distant with co-workers. Everyone he came in contact with shuddered at the idea of having to ask him for help.

One day an interesting thing happened. He broke his leg and wasn't able to come to work. He continued to work from home, but soon he returned full time, using a scooter to make his way around the office. Oddly, I noticed how happy and more responsive he was to his co-workers. Why? I wondered. Then I realized that what he was putting into the universe was coming back to him like a boomerang. His co-workers were concerned, so he mirrored that back. When negativity poured out from him, that's exactly what he'd received as well. I'm not sure he made this connection for himself, but it was a good lesson for those who did see it. When you treat others with respect, then that's what life offers back to you.

I once attended a business networking meeting at a friend's insistence. I had figured it would be your typical meeting where know-it-alls from all walks of life gathered to boast about their credentials. Instead, I was impressed to find business owners who genuinely cared about helping other entrepreneurs find clients. Their goal was to give each other referrals that boosted business. While this practice is not a new phenomenon, to me it felt refreshingly different from the typical corporate work environment. It felt as if everyone was connected in a deep, unconscious way, and no egos were involved judging whether one person was better than another. Everyone was an equal, and know-it-alls were not invited.

In that moment, I realized that corporate America could take a lesson from this way of doing business: helping each other, rather than promoting constant competition, a race to get ahead at all costs. In a nurturing environment, empathy, kindness, and respect would set the tone, making the work environment much more pleasant.

Interestingly, an attorney approached me at the end of the networking meeting with a referral for my publishing business. I was once again surprised to find a person I had judged to be a know-it-all, simply by his profession, to be the exact opposite: caring, inspiring, and willing to share his success.

I realized that just because someone is smart, it doesn't necessarily make them a know-it-all. And just because they are a know-it-all, it doesn't necessarily make them smart.

Oops, I'm the know-it-all. Now what?

Not one person at work, but several, have made comments about your know-it-all manner. You've finally come to the grim realization that deep down, your behavior is a coping mechanism that keeps people from getting to know the real, vulnerable you. You fear that people will find out something that can be used against you, or maybe you're nervous because you're not good at co-worker relationships, and giving attitude masks your true feelings. You think that if you appear as if you know everything, people will think highly of you. But that backfires all too often, and you sense that co-workers feel distanced and aggravated. Maybe on some level you've even felt comforted by telling yourself their feelings are their own fault.

If this description hits the nail on the head for you, then you can bet your ego has been front and center. The good news is you can take action to move it to the side.

What can you do to change your behavior and the impression you make on co-workers? Next time a co-worker is explaining a problem, take time to actively listen. Put yourself in their shoes. Expand your thought process to include what others may be thinking or feeling. When you do this, you naturally move toward allowing others to contribute at work in a meaningful way. Your co-workers can then express their views without fear of retribution. The goal is for everyone to share ideas, and work to complement each other, rather than run roughshod over each other.

Another thing you can do to turn around your behavior: take time to learn about a co-worker's expertise. You'll gain greater respect and appreciation for what they do and endure during a work day. Asking appropriate questions of a co-worker is also a great way to show a caring attitude.

Don't be surprised if it takes co-workers time to come to terms with your new perspective, but eventually they will gain greater respect for you.

THREE TIPS FOR HANDLING A KNOW-IT-ALL WITH GRACE

1. When you need to talk to a know-it-all, make sure to have your research done ahead of time so you can speak intelligently about the topic of conversation.

2. Don't be afraid to speak up and counter a know-it-all's remarks in a professional way. It's not a time to be shy.

3. If you're a know-it-all, actively listen, ask questions, and learn about your co-workers. You'll gain their respect as you learn to appreciate them and their work.

\ | /

I HADN'T REALLY

THOUGHT ABOUT

MY HABIT OF

INTERRUPTING UNTIL

I WAS SO BLATANTLY

CALLED OUT ON IT.

/ | \

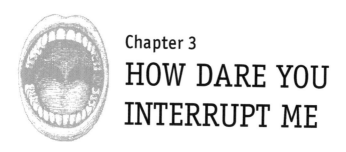

Chapter 3
HOW DARE YOU INTERRUPT ME

I ONCE INTERRUPTED A CO-WORKER SPEAKING TO ANOTHER employee. She screamed at me, "Excuse me, do you mind if I finish my conversation?" Yes, I was the rude interrupter, and I wasn't proud of it.

Frankly, at the time I remember thinking, *Who's the bigger jerk? Me, for interrupting, or her, for screaming at me for a seemingly small infraction?* My justification was that I had an important piece of information to include in their topic of conversation that couldn't wait. Once again, my ego wanted me to believe my ideas were more important. I decided, however, that both of our actions could probably be labeled as workplace conflict.

I hadn't really thought about my habit of interrupting until I was so blatantly called out on it and experienced the results firsthand. I could see my colleague was agitated, and I certainly wasn't feeling good about the situation no matter how I tried to rationalize it. It was not a win-win proposition in the least. But a situation like this is one that sticks in the mind and teaches us to do better.

Not long after, I witnessed another example of how interrupting is problematic in the workplace. I attended a meeting in which everyone was sharing stories to illustrate the topic at hand. They were trying to, anyway. But as time went on, the leader rarely let anyone finish a thought—or start one for that matter. It became evident how damaging it was to the morale of the team. She interrupted time and time again, until a funny thing happened. As sure as hot coffee turns cold, eventually no one would talk or offer any more examples. The leader looked around, perplexed. I sensed that all the participants, other than the leader, knew exactly what had stopped the discussion from playing out to its full potential. They were done and wanted out. Sharing time was over.

There may be a time and place for interruptions. If a co-worker is going off on a tangent or perhaps heading down the wrong road completely, a pause may be in order. But making your point in a kindly manner will make all the difference in moving your work relationship ahead.

I have to admit that after my co-worker yelled at me for interrupting, I was very slow to forgive her for being so crass, even though I deserved it. I later realized that if I'd stopped to listen before chiming in, I would have been seen as a leader and a helpful employee, instead of a hindrance. And it created bad blood, which is never a good move.

Interrupting, in the end, is not listening. It's not giving the person you're speaking with a chance to completely air their side of the story. Important points may be lost if the conversation is intruded on. And sooner or later an interrupter shuts down the conversation completely. Stalemate.

I'm Just Trying to Help

If you are the type of communicator that requires long pauses between thoughts as you process information, you might unknowingly be inviting this interrupting behavior. . . Sometimes people interrupt thinking that a prolonged pause is an invitation to fill in the blank. Or they believe they are helping provide a service to find the words for what they see as you grappling. They fill in the blanks, the voids, the dead air with thoughts they believe you are trying to express.

— Marion Grobb Finkelstein, "Why People Interrupt"

Learning patience and good manners

Interrupting is the selfish person's game. Bad manners? You bet. When you're interrupting, you're thinking only of yourself and what you need to say. You're thinking of answers before they've finished and you're vomiting your wisdom all over them prematurely. This practice leaves little room for being open-minded and conveying a good stream of well-thought-out ideas.

Oh, but it's so easy to interrupt! There probably isn't a person in the world who hasn't done it, and it can be a hard habit to break if done continually. Our minds are thinking a mile a minute, and it's natural to interrupt so as to not forget an idea or thought.

Here's one way to combat being an interrupter: As ideas and counterpoints come to you during a conversation, take quick notes—on your phone or on a piece of paper. That way your idea won't be lost, and at the same time you'll appear more as a considerate professional instead of an interrupting clod.

If you're dealing with a constant interrupter, stop them as they interrupt you and ask them to listen to your whole story before they make any comments or decisions. Yes, yelling at them is one way to help them realize their error, but it's not the best way to facilitate your work relationship. Have patience and empathy. The person you're having the conversation with may not thank you directly, but unconsciously there will be a level of respect gained.

The Golden Nugget

David Nour, author and thought leader on "relationship economics," writes in a blog post titled "I'll Excuse You for Talking While I'm Interrupting": "If a behavior bothers you in other people, take a close look: you probably noticed a trait of your own that is annoying to others."

Take a minute to reflect on this statement. If you're truthful with yourself, can you find some validity in this statement? Try looking at it from a detached, third-party observer role. Can you see the truth? Or does your ego get in the way of finding that golden nugget that would move you towards wisdom and self-realization?

No interrupter in this story

Sometimes we come across people we like and we're not really sure why. I have such a friend. She is kind and expresses her thoughts from a deep well of intuition. These make her great company, but they don't quite hit on the real reason I love to talk to her.

What makes our conversations so extraordinary? I believe it's that she never interrupts, making our exchanges so rich and thoughtful. She allows others to finish thoughts and express them back to her. She truly is a shining example of how conversations should be exercised and it is rare to meet someone like her who allows the flow of conversation to go where it needs to go. I doubt she understands that this tiny practice is worth so much. But then again, she has many friends, so I believe unconsciously the world picks up on her gift.

We need to find ways to communicate that allow each person to have their say. That doesn't mean we have to agree, but it does mean we respect them enough to hear them out entirely before responding. This is where active listening can make a real difference. (Refer to chapter 2, "Excuse Me, Your Big Ego Is Stepping on Mine.") Keeping this in mind during a conversation could mean the difference between someone having a good day or a crummy day.

Not all interruptions are bad

Sometimes life itself is a major interrupter. The alarm clock interrupts the dreams that may have been giving us some much-needed guidance. Bad traffic interrupts the good song on the radio that was making us smile and sing along. A meeting interrupts our efforts to get our true work done. The death of a close friend or family member interrupts our reality and teaches us to look at life a different way.

Interruptions shouldn't be seen as something inherently negative. They can motivate us to look at something in a new light. They can be life's way of teaching us a lesson that we hadn't grasped. Sometimes it takes someone yelling at us, *"Pay attention!"* to force a new perspective.

Other times, taking a vacation is a good way to interrupt the tedium and tension that arise when we've worked too long and too hard without a break. I'm not talking about taking one day off to do our laundry or finally wash and put away the dishes that have been in the sink for weeks. I'm talking about taking a week or two off work to decompress, to travel to another country to experience a different culture than our own and gain a new perspective on our own lives. It is amazing after a well-deserved break how the dark cloud above your head that is causing misery seems to dry up and things that were significant and consuming just aren't that important anymore. We gain a new understanding on life. When we return to work, we can feel joy again, and the things that bothered us previously don't seem to rub us the wrong way anymore.

I'm often humbled at how life's lessons come to me. It's usually not in a manner I would have expected. But when something causes tension, creates anger, or agitates the soul, there's usually a practical and needed message hiding in it: a rose among the thorns.

Whether you look at the interruption experience as something to learn from, or you become bitter, it is up to you. Like my co-worker interruption experience, it could have been so easy for me to hold a grudge. So many times people complain and try to pawn it off as the other person's fault. But instead, try these steps:

1. Stop a moment.
2. Take time to digest the situation.
3. Process the lesson.
4. Realize how you handled the situation may not have been the best, or there were other options that could have been chosen.
5. Forgive yourself.

After going through this process, you may start to have a small inkling of your own inner power to forgive and forget. You have the choice to consciously change your behavior patterns and make new, better ones.

 ## THREE TIPS FOR DEALING WITH THE IRRITATION OF INTERRUPTIONS

1. Ask the interrupter to kindly hear you out before providing a response. Let the person know that when they don't listen fully, it hurts the business at hand.

2. If someone is a habitual interrupter, suggest that they jot notes down so they can remember their ideas and mention them later.

3. Notice the various kinds of interruptions in your life. Take the time to look for the benefits and the lessons to be learned.

\ | /

IN PERSON I COULD

TELL HE HAD A GOOD

HEART, BUT HIS

EMAILS CERTAINLY

DIDN'T GIVE HIS

SECRET AWAY.

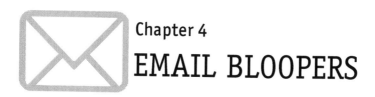

Chapter 4

EMAIL BLOOPERS

T RYING TO MAKE COMPLETE SENSE OF IMPAIRED, quasi-professional emails can be a tough job. I've found a lot of email dominated by run-on sentences, casual-speak, misspelled words, and online chat abbreviations, all making a mess out of a simple sentence. AND IF THAT ISN'T BAD ENOUGH, EVERYTHING IS IN CAPITAL LETTERS SO I CAN'T TELL WHETHER IT'S IMPORTANT OR BECAUSE THE STUPID CAPS LOCK IS STUCK ON!

Back in the 1990s, when email emerged in the workplace, the world was more forgiving. Employees didn't know the first thing about what was deemed acceptable, and what was rude, when writing a professional email.

The email world was the wild, wild West and anything was acceptable—all caps, sentences put together with no punctuation or division of thoughts, and colorful backgrounds with unreadable fonts.

But some twenty-five years later, email etiquette, it could be argued, is in as much disarray as when it first began. Today we still find some of the same transgressions showing up, with many new ones sneaking in to stir the pot.

Here is the interesting part. In the early 1990s, each person typically sent only a handful of messages per day. As of 2010, however, more than 294 billion messages are piped through the internet *each day*—equating to a massive 2.8 million emails sent every second. That's an incredible amount of communication—or potentially disastrous miscommunication—being distributed.

It doesn't take a rocket scientist to see that how we communicate professionally is more important than ever. Employees have less and less time to read because of the constant bombardment of written material. That's not even counting the tidbits of news we read, the social media posts, and of course, the general web content. It's no wonder we often feel overwhelmed with information.

Inappropriate email etiquette can strain work relationships. A poorly written message takes twice as long to read, taking up precious time in which other work could be done. Co-workers can also find it difficult to judge the writer's tone or interpret the real meaning behind their words.

Swearing, belittling, and oversharing about your private life is also unprofessional in workplace communication and can cause tension in a work relationship. Proper email etiquette requires thinking about how your message will be received before you hit the Send button.

What many people don't realize is that the tone of a message influences how it will be interpreted by the recipient. If an email doesn't communicate its message clearly in both tone and specific content, readers will have to use their own judgment to interpret its deeper meaning or intention. And that means they often automatically insert their own fears, prejudices, past experiences, and worries, which can scramble the message.

This Might Not Be Legal

For humorous and sometimes startling examples of email bloopers, check out ThinkBeforeYouSend.com, and David Shipley and Will Schwalbe's book *Send*. Here's an excerpt from chapter 6, "The Email That Can Land You in Jail," courtesy of Cataphora, a company that helps lawyers look for and analyze emails for legal purposes.

"Stupid (and Real) Email Phrases That Wound Up in Court."
1. DELETE THIS EMAIL!
2. Do NOT tell Joe.
3. Can we get away with it?
4. They'll never find out.
5. I have serious concerns.
6. I don't care what the hell you do.
7. This might not be legal.

As we communicate with people from diverse backgrounds and cultures, proper email etiquette becomes even more crucial. Language and cultural differences can be significant barriers to understanding between co-workers, between business colleagues, and between business representatives and customers. Sending inappropriate or error-ridden emails can lead to a host of problems that can cost money, lose business, and strain relationships.

Hiding behind an email

One major offense is writing something in an email that you would never say to someone's face. While it could be appreciated they got to the point, email should never be the place where you get up the nerve to dump and run. As Shipley and Schwalbe explain, "On email, people aren't quite themselves: they are angrier, less sympathetic, less aware, more easily wounded, even more gossipy and duplicitous. Email has a tendency to encourage the lesser angels of our nature."

I worked with a guy who often wrote in such a way that his messages came off as condescending, and messages that he didn't really mean seeped into his words. In addition, he committed many common errors such as misspellings, missing words, and run-on sentences. Being new to the company, I wondered why he was so demeaning when he emailed, because when I talked with him in person, he was friendly and approachable. In person I could tell he had a good heart, but his emails certainly didn't give his secret away. Somehow I don't think he understood the extent to which his emailing etiquette put others off and created discord within his whole department, even though managers tried repeatedly to put his actions on notice. He ended up coming dangerously close to being fired.

Another email transgression I encounter all too often is an overly familiar tone with a co-worker or client, sometimes supplemented with jokes or cartoons. While these can add humor and a level of closeness to a work relationship, they can also easily cross the line into harassment.

I worked with a vendor who, while he was a little rough around the edges, generally got the job done on time. During the course of a project, I had followed up and asked him if a job was on track for the deadline he'd originally agreed to. In an email, he told me that someone at his office hadn't followed his instructions and now the job was in jeopardy of being late, adding "wtf" (short for "what the f**k"). I felt uncomfortable just reading it. Swear words have no business showing up in professional emails. Being thoughtful about our word choices is crucial to maintaining good relationships with our co-workers, colleagues, and customers.

Another email faux pas that is often overlooked is sending an email to a long list of *outside* recipients—people outside the workplace—with every email address visible to the whole group.

It's perfectly acceptable to show a list of *internal* recipients' email addresses. But, for example, imagine you're a purchaser sending a quote request to a number of vendors—people who are likely competitors. Showing *that* list of recipients is probably a bad idea. Instead, the email should be addressed to yourself, the author, and blind-copied to everyone else. Just because you have access to someone's email address doesn't mean you should broadcast it for the world to see. What if one of the people you sent the quote to was the CEO of a large corporation who didn't particularly want their competition to have that private piece of information? While I understand not everyone may be aware of this technique, it is worth understanding that it could potentially open the door to unwanted behavior. Information that is given privately should be kept private, unless communicated otherwise.

Another devious habit is to "cc" (courtesy copy) every Tom, Dick, and Sally, usually for one of several purposes: to get a co-worker in trouble, to show off (misguidedly sharing a "mission accomplished" message with a large group), or to fend off accusations of keeping vital information away from the people who need it. This kind of email practice usually stems from insecurities about the employee's status, job performance, or even their relationship with a supervisor.

Recently, a co-worker pointed out a minor typo I had made, copying his whole department on the email. I felt this was a bully tactic and responded, to the whole department, "I am sorry for my transgression and I'm in the process of sending flowers with an apology note." One of the department members messaged me privately: *"Nice job, I don't know why he has to be such a bully—he does that to everyone."* Sometimes publicly admitting that you made an error, that you are human, is enough to silence a co-worker who's overly critical, causing their maneuver to backfire.

Combating email woes

In the professional world, I recommend these defensive actions when emailing:

1. Include an appropriate salutation (Hi, Good morning, etc.).
2. Include the person's name you're writing the message to.
3. Get to the point quickly. (As a guideline, be sure to answer the questions: Who? What? When? Where?)
4. Avoid emoticons (e.g., smiley face) and text speak (e.g., LOL).
5. If writing isn't your strength—or even if it is—keep your sentences simple and direct. Don't try to use obscure vocab-

ulary or jargon. If it's an important message, ask a colleague you trust to read it before you send it.

6. Copy only those who need to take action or need to be informed. (Address participants in alphabetic order or by ranking in the company.)

7. If your email will build on a thread of previous messages, create it using "Reply all" or "Forward" so the message history is retained.

8. If you're emailing a customer or outside business partner or vendor, include your name, phone number, and address of the company you represent.

9. Use your email program's spellchecker. Proofread your message at least once.

It is amazing how many people ignore these tested rules. If you leave out your phone number in your signature, it costs time looking up that information. If people are copied who don't need the information (and bosses copied because of office politics), more time and attention is wasted. If an earlier message that's referred to in the current one isn't included, no one can follow the thread. And the list goes on.

Taking a moment to double-check that important elements in an email are included and clearly presented can make all the difference in terms of successful communication. And if it's a customer or a valued business contact, you don't want them to be frustrated or offended because of an email faux pas. Sooner or later, they'll turn to another company that they see as more professional or trustworthy.

Autocorrect is another wonderful invention that can trip you up if you're not careful, especially when responding to an email from your phone. One day at work I received an email from a manager from another department that read *"Have you no mercy?*" All sorts of worrisome thoughts went through my head as I tried to figure out what the heck I did to deserve this email. Then I figured out what he actually meant: *"Have you no merch?"* "Merch" is the name of a weekly merchandise-related project, and he was merely wondering if we had the items ready to go. Big difference!

Writing for Your Reader

Readers appreciate a straightforward approach. Say simply what you have to say, and then stop. Avoid jargon, buzz words, and paralegal or bureaucratic phrases.

Try to capture the attitude you'd take if your reader were sitting across from you and you were talking.

Keep an eye on the I's in your writing; add you's as often as you can. Move the spotlight from yourself to your reader... Instead of: *I need cooperation to make this work*, write, *Your cooperation can make this work.*

—Ellen Roddick, *Writing That Means Business*

HR and management's role in email issues

One method of dealing with email issues is for human resources staff or management to talk to offenders about their email etiquette as situations arise. The offender may have no idea of the infraction and may welcome a chance to improve. Sometimes workers who haven't been in the email game as long as others just don't know the rules. Another helpful tool is an HR-issued list of do's and don'ts that communicate clear email standards for everyone: longtime employees, as well as new workers.

One way HR staff can check a potential employee's email skills before hiring (especially if that person deals with clients and outside vendors) is to have a candidate compose an email answering a sticky question in thirty seconds. While you may think that a resume or a cover letter would be a good sample of their writing skills, it might not be the most accurate indicator. Considering the many services that help potential candidates write business correspondence, that beautifully written cover letter just might be someone else's words.

A little empathy goes a long way

If you feel a co-worker struggles with their email writing skills, offer to proofread an email that is difficult to write, is sensitive in some way, or is delivering bad news. At my office, I often partner with a co-worker to proof each other's emails, especially if it pertains to delicate information and we're not sure if the message would be received as it was intended. Getting another viewpoint can save a lot of embarrassment.

Hold yourself to high standards

As a rule, keep emails professional, especially when you're addressing a disagreement. Remember, your words will live forever on the email server. Anyone can pick up your writing and use it for or against you, and it can't be taken back. When having a problem with a co-worker, it is always best to pick up the phone and call, or better yet talk in person. Written communication doesn't always successfully convey things like sarcasm, emphasis, irony, or even sympathy or personal warmth, and if your writing is not up to par, your well-intended effort can make you appear less professional. A note of caution: wait until your emotions have simmered down before talking with someone in person, so more misunderstandings aren't added to the fire.

There are times when it's not possible to talk in person because of location. At that point it might be best to write the email, but don't send it right away. That will give you time to process what you're feeling, and further research the problem and look for possible solutions. When there's less emotion, go back to the email, reread it, then edit and send it off.

Lastly, be as honest as possible when emailing. Clients and co-workers can usually sense the hidden message, and if they think you're using "weasel words" to cover something up, it can backfire.

THREE TIPS FOR IMPROVING EMAIL IQ

1. Help a co-worker understand that sending a poorly worded email can hurt feelings inadvertently. Ask them to put themselves in the reader's shoes before hitting the Send button.

2. When emailing a co-worker or a client, being pleasant and direct is a good policy. Swearing, belittling, and referring to your private life don't belong in workplace email.

3. If there is a possibility of misunderstanding, instead of sending an email, talk it through with the person if possible. Face to face, or by phone, is usually better than the confusing process of reading between the lines of an inadequately written email.

\ | /

YES, TEASING CAN

MEAN YOU'RE LIKED,

THAT YOU'RE ONE OF

THE TEAM, BUT MORE

OFTEN THAN NOT IT

CONTAINS A DIG THAT

THE SPEAKER

BELIEVES IS TRUE.

Chapter 5

THE GOOD, THE BAD, AND THE MEAN

T ODAY, WITH SO MANY SENSITIVITY TRAINING programs addressing diversity and discrimination in the workplace, it is amazing that racist, sexist, and degrading remarks still manage to be spoken out loud. Lobbing such remarks is considered a serious offense, and if you're a participant in this activity, you could find your box of belongings briskly handed to you as you're escorted out the door.

In the late 1990s, many companies saw the need for some type of employee training to clarify what constitutes discrimination and harassment. The training was meant to proactively talk with employees about what types of behavior would not be tolerated and how to report a claim for harassment and discrimination. Nothing like this had formally been done before. Thus was born discrimination, diversity, and sensitivity training.

Dr. Susan Strauss, a harassment and bullying consultant, says, "While training is not specifically required by law, the law does require organizations to 'prevent' harassment and discrimination, which includes training. One jury awarded the plaintiff an additional million dollars because the company did not train their employees, particularly managers. Also, the majority of claims to the EEOC (Equal Employment Opportunity Commission) during 2015 are now retaliation at 43 percent, followed by race at 35 percent, and sex and disability at 29 percent."

According to the EEOC, retaliation is defined this way: "An employer may not fire, demote, harass or otherwise 'retaliate' against an individual for filing a charge of discrimination, participating in a discrimination proceeding, or otherwise opposing discrimination. The same laws that prohibit discrimination based on race, color, sex, religion, national origin, age, and disability, as well as wage differences between men and women performing substantially equal work, also prohibit retaliation against individuals who oppose unlawful discrimination or participate in an employment discrimination proceeding."

To learn more about what constitutes retaliation, how to prevent it, and why it happens, take a look at the article "Retaliation: Making It Personal" in the summer 2015 issue of the *Federal Manager*. It contains eye-opening details on what can happen when bruised egos seek revenge.

Crossing the line

Bullying by definition is a form of nonphysical violence or psychological violence, and it is similar to an abusive relationship that traps victims into emotional desolation. Bullying can cross the line into harassment if the perpetrator is motivated by the victim's protected status: factors such as age, nationality, gender, religion, race, heath status, disability or military service. Bullying inflicted on people in these protected classes is illegal harassment and can be grounds for legal action. General bullying is not illegal, although of course it contributes to an offensive work environment.

Because of bullying in schools, bullying in the workplace is now being taken more seriously. A battle is now brewing in employment law on the state level as an increasing number of states consider anti-bullying legislation that would allow workers to pursue medical expenses and lost wages and benefits via lawsuits, which would force employers to review their abusive work environment policies. Once laws begin to be passed, it will likely cause a domino effect and other states will follow.

Who Is the Biggest Bully?

According to a 2014 workplace survey by the Workplace Bullying Institute, 27 percent of US workers have reported being subjected to workplace abuse and an additional 21 percent are witness to bullying.

That's 65.5 million workers affected by bullying. Also, it was found that 69 percent of the bullies were male and 31 percent were female; 60 percent of the targets were women. Women who bullied chose other women to bully 68 percent of the time. What stopped the bullying? Nearly half—48 percent—of the bullied targets resigned their jobs, in some cases because they were forced to quit.

One area that can appear harmless enough, but can quickly turn into quicksand, is innocent teasing. Yes, teasing can mean you're liked, that you're one of the team, but more often than not it contains a dig that the speaker believes is true. It can be an underhanded way of revealing that they dislike you for some reason, and that you're different or inferior in some way to them. In the end, it can strain work relationships, especially if a negative message is repeated over and over.

Are You in a Hostile Work Environment?

The US Department of Labor defines "hostile work environment" this way:

A hostile environment can result from the unwelcome conduct of supervisors, co-workers, customers, contractors, or anyone else with whom the victim interacts on the job, and the unwelcome conduct renders the workplace atmosphere intimidating, hostile, or offensive. Examples are: discussing sexual activities, telling off-color jokes, unnecessary touching, commenting on physical attributes, displaying sexually suggestive or racially insensitive pictures, using demeaning or inappropriate terms, using indecent gestures, using crude language, sabotaging the victim's work, and engaging in hostile physical conduct.

Here's an example of teasing that happened at my office one day. One of my co-workers was diligently helping someone with a project when a woman in his department walked by his office and made a comment, "There's dumb and dumber." He happened to hear what she said and confronted her about it. She said she was just kidding, but offered no apology. To make matters worse, another worker in the office also heard the remark and was so offended she told the boss about the unwelcome, offensive conduct. The boss brushed the whole incident off as a minor infraction—never saying a word to the offender and never speaking to the victim.

In the end, it hurt a lot of feelings and created mistrust. This incident could have escalated and led to an HR intervention. And the worst part is that without any rules about how to deal with this type of behavior, the offender could assume it was acceptable.

Talking before thinking: A recipe for trouble

Every once in a while an incident takes place that makes you wonder, *Why on earth did they say that?* Or, *Did that really just come out of their mouth, or am I hearing things?*

My client (white man), his client (African-American woman), and I (white woman) met for lunch one day to talk about a project we were all working on together. Since we all lived in different cities and came from different backgrounds, it made for an interesting conversation. Since the other woman and I enjoy traveling, we shared stories about our adventures.

My client suddenly blurted out that he didn't like working with black people because he grew up on the rough side of Philadelphia and had had bad experiences.

We both shrank down in our seats, speechless. *Why would he say that to his own client?* I wondered. Was he feeling left out or powerless? In any case, he had voluntarily exposed his normally buried prejudices. Needless to say, that was the last time he ever visited our plant, and the last time his client did business with him again.

Defining Sexual Harassment

According to the US Equal Employment Opportunity Commission, sexual harassment can occur in a variety of circumstances including but not limited to these:

1. The victim as well as the harasser may be a woman or man. The victim does not have to be of the opposite sex.
2. The harasser can be the victim's supervisor, an agent of the employer, a supervisor in another area, a co-worker, or a non-employee.
3. The victim does not have to be the person harassed but could be anyone affected by the offensive conduct.
4. The harasser's conduct must be unwelcome, severe and/or pervasive enough that it interferes with their ability to do their job, and creates a hostile work environment.

Some offenses are more pointedly personal. I'll never forget the day I was eight months pregnant with my first child and I was trying to get a job scheduled for my client at work. Of course, we had to crowbar it in somewhere because the schedule was full. This was our biggest client, so we had to make it work. The irritated scheduler walked into my office and said to me, half-kidding, "I liked you a lot better before you were pregnant—at least you were something to look at." After more than twenty years I still remember that conversation as if it were yesterday.

Wow. I had to sit with that one for a minute. Completely degrading? Absolutely. Even if he didn't really mean it, that is not something that should be said out loud, especially to a hormonal pregnant woman. I went into the bathroom and cried, then worked up the nerve to tell the owner of the company. A half an hour later, the scheduler offered me an apology. Unfortunately, incidents like this stick like a boot in mud in our memory and forever change our work relationships. It wasn't long after that I left the company.

The cousins you don't want to know

Swearing is another bad habit that rears its ugly head in the office. An occasional small burst of seedy language might be forgivable, but when it's used in every other sentence, it's time for a heart-to-heart talk so the behavior is put on notice.

A close cousin to swearing is offensive name-calling, and it can happen at all levels. At one office, an employee tells me, her boss calls people "stupid"—to their faces and behind their backs. Unfortunately, bullying, poor management, and incivility is not illegal unless it is directed toward someone because of their protected class. Everyone should be entitled to their say without fear of retribution, as long as what is being said is respectful toward others. As a manager or owner, if you feel a person has unproductive ideas, then take them off the payroll for that reason—after due process, of course. Remember, if you're the one who hired them, it comes back to you to make it right.

Finding grace in the situation

If you find someone always stomping on your ego, then try having a private conversation with them. Sometimes people don't realize they've hurt your feelings. You may be sad, angry, or quiet at the office, but if you don't speak up, they'll never know an issue is brewing. Maybe they need a wake-up call to help them understand and appreciate your view, and it might put them on notice that their poor behavior is affecting you negatively. People don't read minds, so being direct, but not emotional, is a good route. If you can't leave emotion, tears, and anger out of the equation, it might be best to wait until you can talk about the problem in a more balanced and less damaging way.

Speaking with the culprit may also enlighten you on why their behavior is taking place. Once, when I was having issues with someone I generally enjoyed working with, we sat down and talked about why his attitude had changed. He confessed the reason he was being a jerk had nothing to do with me. He was having marital problems and the stress leaked into his work relationships. Sometimes having someone to talk to is a great relief and diffuses the conflict.

There's always the possibility that you've made a problem worse in your own mind than what it actually is. Giving someone a second chance might be worthwhile, especially if the offender is normally a decent person to work with. Stepping back and taking time to think about the situation also can provide some clarity.

If possible, it's best to first try to work out a problem by directly communicating with your co-worker. But if the problem doesn't get resolved—say, the person is refusing to change their behavior—it may be time to elevate the complaint to your supervisor. If the problem is with an employee whose rank is higher than yours—from your manager on up to the president—then it's time to go to Human Resources. A refresher session in sensitivity training may do the trick. If that doesn't work, then keep in mind that making continuous inappropriate remarks, especially to a person from a protected class (age, nationality, gender, religion, race, heath status, disability, military service) can be grounds for firing. Corporations open themselves up to a lawsuit if these kinds of patterns are ignored.

Illness bullying

Coping with cancer and other major illnesses, parenting a sick child, or even being pregnant and taking maternity leave takes a toll at work as co-workers struggle to do their own job as well as the work of their absent colleague. Workers with an illness, or who are taking care of someone ill, may show up late, miss workdays to visit the doctor, and often aren't able to function physically and emotionally at a normal capacity when they are at work. Snide remarks are heard as the person filling in is asked to do more work for the same pay. Judgments surface: "He's probably faking being sick to get out of work" or "Chemo can't be that bad" or "Her kid is sick *again*—can't someone else take care of him?" It's easy to see why illness bullying has become a new trend.

Illness bullying can go to extremes: co-workers might judge the sick person's treatment methods or how much they talk about the illness. When the person with the illness changes in demeanor and physical appearance, co-workers may intentionally or unintentionally make fun of them.

While it can be difficult for a company to maintain an even keel when a key person is out, think about what the ill person is going through. Maintaining a job may be easy compared to the battle that person is enduring. They may be wondering how they will pay the massive hospital bill, who will care for their loved ones when they are sick, or whether they'll have enough money to pay for basic living expenses. And with a terminal illness, they are likely grappling with their own mortality. If you were to walk in their shoes for even a short time, you would see it is understandable that work is not foremost on their mind.

Showing compassion, respecting the person's privacy, and being aware of the hardships they're coping with all go a long way toward helping someone who is ill, or has an ill loved one, get through the hard times. Sometimes just telling the person you've got everything handled while they are out is a huge relief. As for the extra work, don't be afraid to ask for help from your manager, especially if the load begins to unbalance you.

Writing the wrongs

Another way to diffuse internal anger is to start a journal. Go ahead and label it "Stuff That Makes Me REALLY, REALLY Mad!" In fact, that's exactly how I started this book. When emotions bubbled to the surface and I felt I couldn't say anything to the culprit, I began to write. I had already discussed co-worker issues with my supervisor and he hadn't done anything to control the situation, so I felt as if I was at the end of my rope. Journaling helped. I let everything pour out as if no one would ever read it. Typos, messy handwriting, and swearing were all acceptable.

At first my thoughts were angry and my writing portrayed someone who was hurt, confused, and generally disgusted with corporate America. I wrote everything that came to mind and blamed everyone for their poor behavior. But as I began to write on a daily basis, a 360-degree view of the situation began to come into focus. This allowed compassion and reasoning to enter, and for the first time I could see how my actions and words interplayed with the situation. I realized I needed to take ownership of my actions, which was all I could do anyway. Journaling helped me move to a more peaceful state.

CM Smith, in an article called "6 Ways Journaling Will Change Your Life," says "The simple act of writing a few words, sentences, or paragraphs everyday can have a profound and instant effect on your life for the better. Journaling can change your life and make you more interested and interesting through the years." Here are Smith's six benefits of journaling:

1. Discover how you really feel inside which leads to a deeper and more realistic view of your feelings.
2. Provides another point of view to the situation.
3. Writing "My Life Story" can help you realize how interesting and deep your life is.
4. You get to know the real you, not the personality that comes out in public.
5. Write as a legacy to your ancestors.
6. Helps you process events and builds serenity and balance.

The guiding light

Harassment, discrimination, and insensitivity affect everyone—directly and indirectly—and it should be taken seriously. A corporation's guiding light, its north star, must be to treat each person with respect. Personal dignity comes first. If that tone is set at the highest level—including the CEO—the trickle-down effect helps ensure that managers and employees will follow.

But if rights are encroached upon, then escalation may be the only way to right a wrong. "An employer can be responsible for the acts of a harassing employee if it fails to take immediate, appropriate action once it knows about the harassment," says Marilyn Lindblad in her article "What Is Considered Workplace Harassment?" "Employees who are victims of harassment are encouraged to report the incidents to a supervisor, and many employers publish anti-harassment policies that explain whom to go to with a harassment claim. When the harasser is the victim's supervisor, the employee may report harassment to a senior supervisor, a human resources professional or a government agency."

If you have a specific question about workplace etiquette and the subtle issues of behavior, check out *Ask Sue*, Sue Morem's weekly advice column on the Career Know-How website. Her column deals with professionalism, etiquette, and problems in the workplace, covering a wide range of work issues: what to do if your co-worker wears too much perfume, how to cope with a co-worker who's the boss's best friend, how to handle being passed up for a promotion, and much more.

Think. Consider others' feelings. Then talk. That's how we stay out of the courtroom and in the good graces of others.

THREE TIPS FOR MANAGING THE MEAN

1. Pull the offender aside and talk to them about the issue. Sometimes pointing out a behavior will make it stop.

2. Look at your own sensitivity levels. Try seeing the situation as a bad move on a co-worker's part and just get on with your day.

3. If all avenues have been tried and have failed, ask Human Resources if a sensitivity training session might be in order to refresh the current state of the union. If it's beyond that, then you'll need to ask for more drastic measures.

\ | /

THE WORD "UNCOMFORTABLE"

DOESN'T EVEN BEGIN TO

DESCRIBE THE FEELING WHEN A

COLLEAGUE PULLS YOU INTO

THEIR OFFICE TO SHOW

YOU SOMETHING THEY THINK

IS ENTERTAINING ON

THEIR COMPUTER MONITOR,

ONLY FOR YOU TO BE TOTALLY

EMBARRASSED.

/ | \

Chapter 6

SURFING AT THE OFFICE WITHOUT GETTING WET

DID YOU SEE THAT VIDEO OF THE SKATEBOARDER WHO takes a hilarious fall while attempting a brilliant maneuver off a railing? Or how about the one with the bear that climbs into a backyard pool and floats around as if it owns the place? Lots of laughs are only a click away.

There are literally millions of hilarious—and offensive—videos and web posts that draw our attention away from work. They were produced for that very reason: to amuse, distract, and possibly educate. But it's truly aggravating to sit next to a co-worker at the office who's laughing at something "amusing" when you're trying to get work done.

Sure, there's an overabundance of ways to use up valuable company time courtesy of the internet: shopping, messaging friends, looking up photos of colleagues (oops—that's called networking), not to mention "research," which includes nothing to do with the task at hand. And of course the internet also includes a vast array of rude and offensive pictures, cartoons, and pornographic material. The word "uncomfortable" doesn't even begin to describe the feeling when a colleague pulls you into their office to show you something they think is entertaining on their computer monitor, only for you to be totally embarrassed.

How it all began

The term "surfing" the internet was created by a New York librarian, Jean Polly, aka Net-mom. Polly coined the phrase in 1992 when writing a beginner's level article on using the web. "In casting about for a title for the article, I weighed many possible metaphors," she said. "I wanted something that expressed the fun I had using the Internet, as well as hit on the skill, and yes, endurance necessary to use it well. I also needed something that would evoke a sense of randomness, chaos, and even danger. I wanted something fishy, net-like, nautical."

Little did anyone realize how net-surfing—and Polly's word for it— would become ingrained in our daily lives. Soon, the internet was no longer just a place to look something up. It had morphed into a phenomenon that changed society as we knew it. It gave us our news and weather, showed us how to use videos for entertainment and educational purposes, revealed ways to communicate with others across the globe, and assisted us in navigating from one place to another. In short, our lives became entwined with the internet. Later, internet-connected phones changed the landscape even further.

This fact also accounts for the reason we have such a difficult time resisting the urge to peek at the internet over and over while we're at work. We've become a society that uses the internet for everything. It's no wonder we find it hard to disconnect and focus on work. So what do companies do? Monitor and reprimand employees, or allow some surfing and hope employees don't abuse the rules? There's no hard and fast answer. It falls to each business to create a plan of action and stand by its rules.

Big brother is watching

Nothing surfed on the web at work is private, so it's best to use common sense when it involves the internet. Know that all websites you visit at work are logged, and anyone in IT and management can see what you're viewing. Even activities that aren't offensive, if done for extended amounts of time, could be grounds for admonishment. Some companies monitor your web activity regularly, but not all have the staff resources for that. Still, don't think you're getting by off scot-free. There's no doubt your co-workers have some idea how much time you spend on the web. Keeping your searches work-related and short will gain you respect in the office in the long run.

And beware that clicking on certain links can open the company up to viruses (mischievous code that copies itself), malware (software designed with malicious intent), and ransomware (code that hijacks your data and computer access and requires payment to recover it). Any one of these maladies requires valuable IT time, and sometimes a lot of money, to fix.

IT manager Jeff Jacobson, explains the pitfalls of viruses. "Viruses present the highest security risk for a company. Ironically, each user is the weak link in the equation. Usually a user accidentally allows or invites in a virus. That can happen by opening a tainted email attachment or inserting a corrupt flash drive or even via someone's personal device that's infected when remoting in, which ingeniously infects the whole system."

Jacobson adds, "Viruses aren't small things like they were in the past. Some are designed to pack a punch by propagating through the whole network, some turn the host computer into a mule, others hijack your data, and so on. More and more IT time is spent on prevention, and thinking of ways to block problems before they ever get to the user. The last thing a company needs is for the network to go down, with employees sitting around unable to work or communicate with clients."

A well-documented example occurred in 2014, when Sony Pictures Entertainment and Sony Entertainment's computer network was hacked, thus divulging executive's salaries, revealing yet-to-be-released films, exposing private emails, and demanding that a specific future movie be canceled and not be shown in theaters. Needless to say, the network was shut down, the FBI was called in, and millions of dollars and hours were spent trying to trace and identify the hacker, rectify the situation, manage the fallout, and install preventative measures. Not only was the hack damaging monetarily, it also created distrust, fear, and loss of proprietary information.

The gray zone

With company-owned laptops and phones being used at the workplace and elsewhere, a gray area presents itself. In these instances, most workers use their devices for personal as well as business purposes, unless the company has strict policies in place. But imagine you're on your way home, wearing a shirt with your company logo embroidered on the pocket. You're stuck at the subway terminal, so you decide to pull out your laptop, and since you're off duty, you indulge in some questionable material. Now those sitting around you are offended. What do they look at first? The name of your company stitched prominently on your shirt. What does that say about your company and their employee practices? Whether it belongs to you or the company, it's best to use discretion when using any device in public—or anytime, for that matter.

Vaccinate Your Computer

PC World offers these rules to help prevent harm from viruses:

1. Keep your security software, including your firewall, up to date.
2. Keep your browser up to date.
3. If a browser warns you that a page is dangerous, don't visit that page, even if you know it's owned by trustworthy people. If you can get a message to those people without visiting the site, let them know about the problem.
4. Scan your hard drive regularly with an on-demand security program made by a company that didn't make your regular security software.

If you're really paranoid about a site, either don't go there, or boot a live Linux CD or flash drive and access the site without using Windows.

Jacobson said, "Employees should not have expectations of privacy. As an IT manager, I can see most everything you do on your company phone (if on Wi-Fi), and your company computer. Most employees violate our internet policy by using their computer for personal use. They assume 'it's mine, so I can do what I want.' If the problem persists, I talk to the employee's boss and let them handle it on an individual basis. Employees don't realize, when you look at personal use on a company-wide basis, there is a tremendous amount of time spent not getting their job done."

He adds, "But not everything is set in stone. Many people have the expectation that a certain amount of personal use is acceptable. Policies and 'the gray zone' will continue to change with the times."

Handle the problem with professionalism

What should you do about a co-worker who surfs the internet frequently or watches inappropriate material during work hours? If their activity, or lack of activity, affects you in some way directly, then talking to the boss is a possible solution. The downside is it could make you look like a tattletale.

In some settings, the truth about who's productive always comes out—eventually. In our group, we have a "pool" of work where each member of the team takes another job when they finish a project. Each job written is logged. Eventually, management can view a report that shows each employee's productivity. It becomes obvious who does the work and who doesn't. At this point, it's up to the boss to dig into the reasons a certain level of productivity isn't being maintained. Unless you're called into the manager's office to provide your viewpoint, it's best to stay out of the mess and let the circumstances get handled at a higher level.

One option is to ask the excessive internet user to help you on projects so they don't have time to browse. Maybe your co-worker is bored but chooses to surf rather than looking for a new project. Even if this only works occasionally, perhaps depending on your co-worker's mood, it can give you the satisfaction that you tried. In some environments, sharing projects might not be possible. In that case, try to calm your feelings of annoyance with the thought that what goes around comes around.

What if an employee is looking at offensive material on their work computer? If possible, tell the offender that it's bothering you. What's offensive to one person may simply be funny or merely entertaining to someone else. Try to give your co-worker the benefit of the doubt by talking to them first. If you know it violates company policy, you could let them know so they can avoid being written up. Sometimes just bringing it to their attention alleviates the problem.

If you feel you've made an honest effort to alert the offender to the problem and nothing has changed, then it's time to go to a manager or Human Resources. Companies are usually keenly aware of the potential legal pitfalls, and most will make sure the situation is corrected in some way, whether it's a slap on the wrist or termination.

I'm a surfer and I know it

If you find you have spare time and your go-to activity is web surfing, try breaking the habit by substituting something else. I know for myself when I have down time it's really easy to sneak a peek at web news, so I do my best to have projects lined up to keep me busy. Taking on side projects also says you're an employee who is excited and wants to be at work.

What if you're an overqualified employee who can easily get your work done in half the time, and there just isn't any other work available? Surfing the web, no doubt, is a fun way to fill the time and keeps you from dying of boredom. Instead, what if you asked your manager for web research projects so you could put your skills to good use? Or ask to take an online class that would enhance your professional development and look good on your resume. Looking for creative ways to keep busy while performing work functions you enjoy is a great way to make the work hours go by fast, and you could get noticed for a promotion.

Sure, it's easy to judge your co-workers' actions. But in the end, don't doubt for a moment that if you keep your nose to the grindstone, management and co-workers notice. For every day you do your job without complaining, finger-pointing, or judging, you gain greater respect. And when you're ready to leave that job, not only have you gained the esteem of your co-workers and managers, but they are much more apt to give you a good review or the thumbs-up on being a great employee to work alongside. There's even a possibility that recruiters who've heard of your ethical work practices through the grapevine will come calling.

Be honest, work hard, and forget about what others are doing. Concentrate on what you are doing. And leave the entertainment web surfing for off hours in the privacy of your own home.

THREE TIPS FOR DISCOURAGING THE SURFER

1. Ask an excessive internet user to help you on a project so they don't have time to surf.

2. Tell an offender who continues to embarrass you with offensive material that it's not acceptable. If it continues, let human resources staff know—after you've done everything you can to address the problem.

3. If you continually have excess time and no work, ask your manager for research projects. Or ask if it would be appropriate to take an online class. Look for creative ways to keep busy while performing work functions.

\ | /

BUT WHAT MOST

DEFERRERS AREN'T

PREPARED FOR IS THAT

PROCRASTINATION

AT THE WORKPLACE

PRODUCES A RESULT

THAT EVERYONE

IMMEDIATELY NOTICES:

SLOPPY WORK.

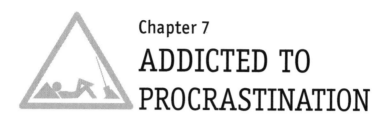

Chapter 7
ADDICTED TO PROCRASTINATION

GET-THINGS-DONE ME: *LET'S ROCK THIS PROJECT AND finish it ahead of time so we can WOW our customer.*

Procrastinator Me: *That's a great idea, but first I need a cup of coffee and a danish from that new cafe down the street. It wouldn't hurt if we started a little later, when I've woken up, right? I guarantee I'll be as productive as a mouse running on a wheel.*

While everyone procrastinates to a certain degree, it is the chronic procrastinator we find troubling. We're talking about people who deceive themselves, saying their outcome will be more creative if they wait, or there are other things more important than the task at hand. It's like watching a game of tennis: back and forth the justifications and lies go. But that's exactly what a procrastinator is clever at doing: making up excuses and stalling. Where some of us may grit our teeth and get the job done whether we feel like it or not, a true procrastinator will justify why something can't be done right now.

Putting things off may seem like an innocent offense, but it can quickly become a habit that can hurt your chances for success at work and slow your corporate climb to the top. When co-workers have a joint project with delegated responsibilities and a clear deadline, they expect each person to do their fair share in a timely manner. It is no fun to present your findings to the boss, or even worse to a client, with a section that has noticeably fallen flat. The one person who procrastinated and failed to add to the project's quality just let the whole team down.

Sometimes it's apparent that one person sabotaged the project and they are held accountable, but other times the whole team may suffer. Now the procrastinator has put everyone's job and reputation on the line.

A procrastinator's habit may have started back in their grade school or high school days. They admirably got that project done in one night and got a decent grade, so it reinforced the behavior. Perhaps they even thought that they wouldn't have done as well if they'd started earlier. They may have even had a good laugh at classmates who started the project three weeks ago and got the same grade.

But what most deferrers aren't prepared for is that procrastination at the workplace produces a result that everyone immediately notices: sloppy work. While getting away with a grade of C in school was "good enough," it didn't earn any gold stars. And that's even more true on the job. Last-minute work will nearly always be subpar. The effort often lacks depth and may not offer solid solutions to the issue at hand.

Frequent sloppy work puts a target on your back. And when layoffs are imminent, guess who's on the chopping block first? Companies can't afford to have employees who just show up for work, never putting forth their best effort.

A Field Guide to Procrastinators

In an interview with *Psychology Today*, psychology professor Joseph Ferrari identifies three types of procrastinators:

- Arousal types, or thrill-seekers, who wait [until] the last minute for the euphoric rush.
- Avoiders, who may be avoiding fear of failure or even fear of success, but in either case are very concerned with what others think of them; they would rather have others think they lack effort than ability.
- Decisional procrastinators, who cannot make a decision. Not making a decision absolves procrastinators of responsibility for the outcome of events.

Being late to work is another type of procrastination that hurts your chances for upward mobility. And for a salaried worker, it actually is a subtle way of stealing from the company. Walking into work half an hour late because of an unexpected accident or a snow storm may not get you hot water, especially if you make up the time later; but if you're frequently late, those around you take notice—including the boss. If there are no consequences, other co-workers have just been given permission to follow your example.

The same goes with being tardy to meetings and appointments. You are unconsciously telling others, who made it to the meeting on time, that you are more important. Where I work, the conference rooms are always booked back to back, so starting late translates into having less time to talk about the task at hand, making meetings rushed and less effective.

How do workers procrastinate?

One reason people put things off is that they're easily distracted. They have poor time-management skills, and something else always seems more important. A good example is the employee who knows the boss has asked for the wrap-up of a certain project, but there always seem to be other projects that take precedence. While those projects may need to be done at some point, a procrastinator may be using them as an excuse to avoid doing the priority project. It also gives them a legitimate excuse to not complete the work. In their mind, the avoided task is an issue that they just can't seem to conquer. The underlying cause may be fear of failure, or an odd kind of perfectionism.

There's always the possibility that a general lack of passion is the key reason for not completing a task. People who procrastinate generally do so on projects they aren't enthusiastic about. If you're doing something you truly love, you're likely to keep at it.

Procrastinators tend to be less wealthy and less healthy. They put off going to the doctor when they know there's a problem or put off looking for another job when they are unhappy. One way a professional procrastinator operates at work is to avoid a conversation about the delayed task. Here's an example: do you have co-workers whose offices are so strewn with piles of paper you can barely step in? And when you mention the issue, they may make a joke about it, or completely ignore the conversation altogether. Even if you point out that management frequently walks clients through their area, and their mess could make the company look bad, they remain in avoidance or denial mode. They may even be ingenious about turning the tables and making you feel bad for bringing it up.

While you could make a case that a person who is messy is a world-class procrastinator, you could also say someone with an immaculate office might also be one. I know for myself when it's time to write something that is difficult and requires hard-core research, I'll procrastinate and do something else that appears to be productive. When I look at what I've accomplished, on the surface it appears I've achieved a mountain of work, but digging deeper I can see I really missed the mark on doing what was truly important.

What to do about a procrastinating colleague

Provide the procrastinator with a deadline. "ASAP" is not good enough. That simply translates to *as soon as I feel like it or get around to it.* Be firm. For myself, if I understand why something is important or has a hot deadline, it makes all the difference in how I will prioritize it, and I'll be less likely to put it on the back burner. When everything is due right now, it soon feels like the boy who cried wolf.

If there's a procrastinator on your team, make a detailed daily plan that outlines what's to be worked on and completed. Micromanaging? You bet. But it's better than being left with all the work the night before the deadline. Don't forget to check up on progress as time passes. Just because a plan is in place doesn't mean it will be followed. The key is to break the plan down into bite-size portions so it looks and feels achievable, not overwhelming.

Are You Addicted to Procrastination?

How do you know if you're procrastinating? *Mind Tools* offers some hints:

1. Filling your day with low priority tasks.
2. Reading e-mails several times without deciding what you're going to do with them.
3. Sitting down to start a high-priority task, and almost immediately going off to make a cup of coffee.
4. Leaving an [important] item on your To Do list for a long time.
5. Regularly saying "Yes" to unimportant tasks instead of getting on with the important tasks already on your list.
6. Waiting for the "right mood" or the "right time" to tackle the important task at hand.

Incentives, too, might push a procrastinator to success. Find out what entices and motivates your co-worker. If it takes a candy bar from the vending machine, you're in luck. If it takes a trip to Hawaii, then, depending on the stakes, you might have some fancy footwork to do to make it happen. If at any time it seems that dangling the carrot has become the norm, otherwise nothing gets done, you might want to consider whether or not your co-worker belongs on the team. It may take a conversation with the boss to find the right solution.

I'm the procrastinator

You've done some soul-searching and made the important realization that you're a procrastinator. Good for you. That's the first step in controlling your addiction. Luckily, there are some steps you can do yourself to lessen your compulsion to defer projects.

Try making a list of things that need to get done at work and check them off as you complete them. Because you made a list and planned, the universe starts working to help you achieve your goals. Make a rule that you can't go home until everything is done. A word of caution: be realistic in your demands. Falling off the wagon, so to speak, will only make you feel inadequate, and soon you'll want to forget the whole thing and go back to your old ways.

Another good technique is to put yourself in your colleagues' shoes. Consider how co-workers feel when you leave a project hanging: now everyone on the team is on the hook for your mistake. In the same breath, don't beat yourself up if you've slipped up. Having a little compassion for yourself, as well as others, will help everyone get along better and ultimately be more productive.

Reward yourself when you've completed the project within the agreed-on time frame. Pat yourself on the back for a job well done. Recognize the small steps in conquering that voice inside that provides bad advice. Remember, that voice can and will do everything in its power to derail your good intentions. Pause for a moment, and just watch how it brings up all sorts of reasons something shouldn't, and can't, be done. Just watch it as if you're watching a bully picking on a kid. That bully is your ego. You, and only you, can choose whether you'll listen.

In the end, procrastination is the soul's way of telling you something isn't right. It may reveal that the type of work you are engaged in leaves you drained rather than energized, and procrastinating is your way of dealing with the problem. Maybe procrastination exposes a glitch in a co-worker relationship, and it's easier to defer your feelings than face them. Figure out and address the real reason behind the procrastination, and it often becomes a minimal problem.

THREE TIPS FOR PROCRASTINATION PREVENTION

1. Make a detailed plan and check off to-do items as they are completed.

2. When faced with a large project, find incentives for others and yourself to keep motivation levels high and procrastination low.

3. Figure out what kind of procrastinator you are—a thrill-seeker, an avoider, or a decisional procrastinator—and plan ahead how you can avoid that tendency when it creeps into a situation. You'll get back on track faster.

\ | /

IT'S TRULY AGGRAVATING

FOR AN EMPLOYEE

WHO IS JUDGED ON

THEIR MERITS TO HAVE

TO DEAL WITH

SOMEONE WHO ISN'T.

/ | \

Chapter 8

MIX FAMILY WITH BUSINESS

STIR, BOIL, THEN PRESSURE COOK

WHETHER YOU'RE A FAMILY MEMBER OR NOT, WORKING for a family firm can be a great, nurturing experience, or it can be downright ugly. In the pleasant scenario, everyone works together like a finely tuned instrument and the business grows. In the unpleasant scenario, family members say things to each other that should never be spoken in a business setting, and they revert back to their childhood days of name-calling and nit-picking.

If you've worked in a family environment with a balanced system and a stable plan of action, count yourself lucky. While it may seem like a win-win, low-risk idea to include trusted family members in a business, sometimes that idea can produce ramifications that impacts the business in a unpredictable way. Depending on how family members interact with each other, those decisions could determine whether employees like or detest their jobs, and whether the business flourishes.

If you've ever worked in a situation where family members don't get along, you know how intensely uncomfortable that can feel. Conflicting viewpoints can especially be cause for concern if an argument goes too far. One family member may venture out of the corporate rules and set their own course into uncharted waters. In turn, employees can become confused about which guidelines to follow, and the ship ends up being divided, with each family member taking as many supporting employees as possible in their own life raft.

I once worked in what I'd call a very dysfunctional family business setting. The kids, eight total, had taken over the company from their parents, who had given everything they had to create a thriving business. This would have been an ideal opportunity to continue the family legacy and tighten the family bonds. Sadly, most of the siblings had wildly differing opinions on how to run the business. Everyone stepped on everyone else's toes (other siblings and employees alike), and soon doors would slam and the yelling ensue.

The word "unnerving" cannot even begin to describe the thick air that enveloped the work area. Can you guess what happened to the business the family had worked so hard to build? Bankruptcy. It wasn't lack of work, or employee talent; it was the family's inability to agree on one guiding force, one set of rules, to live by.

I've also seen family businesses run relatively smoothly as long as each family member held the appropriate position and remained respectful of their siblings as well as other employees. That meant Uncle Bob, an efficient accountant, wasn't trying to blast hip marketing messages on Twitter for the company, and Sister Sue who was well suited as a receptionist wasn't running plant production. While it's understandable that family members in a small organization need to chip in and help where possible, sometimes it's better to outsource tasks that lie outside everyone's skill sets.

Jim Counter, a retired financial business owner who has worked with two family members, agrees it pays to have separate, distinct jobs that take into account each member's strengths. He said, "Family and business don't always mix well, but as the owner I never doubted my family's passion to get us through the hard times. In the end, that is all an owner can ask for—to create something that is continued and taken care of in the same manner as what the owner would have done."

Often, a family is so dedicated to the firm that tasks end up being micromanaged—or perhaps viewed through distorted lenses. Some family members may overlook the errors of others or, on the other end of the spectrum, they may exaggerate those mistakes, sometimes adding fuel to the fire by bringing personal issues into a business argument. Other times, family members may be taken for granted and end up working longer hours than other employees.

A particular challenge arises when a family member uses the "My family owns the business so it doesn't matter if I'm a slacker" card. It's truly aggravating for an employee who is judged on their merits to have to deal with someone who isn't. Hiring someone who can never be fired is a recipe for bad morale. Again, keeping expectations clear will make all the difference.

"As an employer/business owner I look at all of my employees the same way I would my own children," explains Linda Skoglund, president of J.A. Counter. "That may sound strange, but it's true. Just like my kids, they need nurturing, support, encouragement, and rules. They push their boundaries to figure out how far they can go. Mentoring employees is a responsibility that every successful business owner and HR professional must naturally make a part of their day. Managing expectations, whether it be with your family, your co-workers, or your customers, is critical to creating balance."

Listen to your gut

If you're considering working for a family business, if possible check with an ex-employee about their experience. Or if that's not feasible, ask about policies in the interviewing process, and discuss the family dynamic as they see it. You might even ask to meet working family members and try to get an idea of how they interact with each other. If your gut tells you something isn't right, then listen.

What if it's too late? You took that dream job a block from your house for double the pay, and everything seemed rosy and cheery. But eventually the hidden dysfunction makes its way to the forefront. The strategy for survival in this situation is to stay out of family arguments. You may think it's a good move to talk about one family member to another, but you should know they'll always talk to each other (eventually)—even if they're not speaking to each other right at that moment. The wrinkles tend to be ironed out at their Sunday brunch, and you could then be the topic of discussion.

If you're having friction with a certain family member, first talk to them privately. If you're not getting anywhere, you could consider calling a meeting with the rest of the family in the business and explain how that person's behavior is not creating an optimal work environment. This may be a bold move, but depending on your position on the food chain, you might be able to coax family members to act in a more professional, responsible manner.

If that doesn't seem to move them to act more appropriately, then put your head down, focus on work, and update your resume when you're off duty.

In these instances, I find reciting a mantra helps get my mind off moments that test my patience. Take a deep breath, and silently tell yourself, *This too shall pass* or *I am stronger than this situation* or *I choose to be calm.* After a few minutes, you'll feel the stranglehold of the situation lessen, and clarity will come to you. Life lessons are never easily won, especially when you're working through the tough spots. I believe that each person who comes into our life is there for a reason. If you look at these difficult people and circumstances as life lessons, it may help you move to a more detached state.

Helping Family Members Work Together

Brad Walters, CEO of Monnit Corporation, has some tips for effectively managing family members as employees:

- Require the family member to report to somebody apart from you.
- Be open and honest in communicating expectations and providing feedback.
- Differentiate and establish clear boundaries between work and personal life.
- Be open about familial relationships.

Separation of church and state

Or is it you who works alongside a sibling or another relative? Remember that just because you know all the dirt on that person doesn't mean you have the right to fire that ammunition in an argument at work. And don't think that pushing the right buttons to make a family member squirm is ethical, either. Keeping a fair and balanced view can be hard, but keeping work issues separate from personal ones is crucial to a healthy workplace. Separation of church and state, so to speak, is a good policy to follow.

If an argument ensues, and you can't seem to find a way to rectify the situation, then get HR staff involved to act as the neutral mediator. Try to listen to each other in a nonbiased way and see the problem from each other's viewpoint. Agree to work and communicate on a professional level, rather than replaying those old childhood dynamics.

HR's job at this point is to document events, hold members accountable, and check in on the situation from time to time. These steps can help prevent work interruptions or even employee departures because of an unpleasant working environment.

Learn to work together, family or not. No one wants to go to a family gathering and have to deal with unresolved anger and friction spilling over from work. And by the same token, nonfamily employees don't need to hear and be involved in the family's personal issues.

THREE TIPS FOR TOILING IN A FAMILY BUSINESS

1. If you're a nonfamily member working at a family-run business, stay out of family arguments if possible—or talk to family members privately and share your concerns about how their behavior is affecting productivity.

2. If you own a family business, utilize your family members' specific skills, and hire employees or outsource work that doesn't fit family talents.

3. If you are a part of a family business, take disagreements to a private office and discuss solutions away from employees to keep harmony, structure, and morale flowing within the business.

\ | /

SOME PEOPLE ARE

DISTURBED BY HAVING

A CO-WORKER JUST

BRUSH BY THEM IN

A TIGHT SPACE.

/ | \

Chapter 9

SPACE INVADERS ARE HERE!

J UST SO WE'RE CLEAR: LITTLE GREEN ALIENS FROM PLANET Venus are not the subject of this conversation. This chapter is about a different kind of invader, one we see all too often in the broad daylight of the corporate office: people who fail to recognize a co-worker's personal space.

Each person has a different comfort level when it comes to personal space, and those boundaries can change with various people and situations. You might have found this out the hard way, unconsciously stepping into someone's inner, sacred circle and having to deal with their strong reaction.

While some people are offended at the slightest physical closeness, others don't seem to mind a more engaged touch. It's definitely not easy to spell out a hard and fast rule for the workplace.

"This matter of personal space is becoming more of an issue as we become more ethnically diverse," says harassment and bullying consultant Dr. Susan Strauss. "Some ethnicities, for example, normally stand quite close to another person in conversation, while others stay further away and may even avoid eye contact."

One thing is certain: failing to understand and respect personal boundaries can lead to discomfort and tension between co-workers. That tension, if unaddressed, in turn can lead to an unhealthy workplace climate and damage productivity.

Uninvited personal contact: What does that mean exactly? It means a touch that is not wanted. It doesn't necessarily mean intimate or sexual touch—it's just uncomfortable for some reason.

You might wonder why touching someone in a nonsexual manner could be considered offensive. Doesn't it demonstrate to the recipient that they are liked and part of the "friend" network? A good old pat on the back. A slap on the knee. A squeeze of the shoulder. But while it might be okay if my best friend gives me a hug, it might not be okay if the person who works in the next cubicle does the same. That innocent hug can turn into something disturbing faster than you can say "c-r-e-e-p-y."

Like so many work stressors, space invaders are an unwelcomed distraction. You may be less willing to work with a co-worker who makes you feel uncomfortable. More important, if intrusive behavior isn't held in check, it can lead to someone feeling harassed. At this point, we're not talking about an accidental touch. We're talking about continued unwelcomed touch that truly breaches the boundaries of a working relationship. Workers who cross the line could be setting themselves up for dismissal from their job and even a lawsuit. (See chapter 5, "The Good, the Bad, and the Mean.")

Often, space invaders don't realize what they're doing. Perhaps they came from a touchy-feely kind of family and grew up standing close to others. While within the family dynamic this is totally okay—even admirable—at work it's an entirely different ballgame. And the person with the "too-close" habits ends up feeling like a strikeout at the bottom of the ninth, without being sure why. Sometimes, a co-worker who is nervous or attempting to be friendly becomes an unconscious invader. To others, the encounter will feel strange and weirdly unsettling rather than friendly.

Be Conscious of Your Total Environment

In "Respecting a Co-Worker's Personal Space," Lisa McQuerrey advises employees to be mindful of personal grooming and other habits in the workplace:

> While the air your officemates breathe and the sounds they hear may not constitute individual personal space, you can still respect the contribution you make to these intangible shared office assets. Be mindful about how aromatic your food and beverages are and be careful about the amount of perfume or cologne you wear. Likewise, pay attention to your volume when you speak, both in person and on the phone, to ensure you aren't interrupting your colleagues' work or concentration.

Damaging work relationships

Once I was teaching a new employee the processes at our office. While she was intelligent and receptive to learning, she also seemed nervous. Every time she was near me, I'd find her patting my knee or hugging my shoulder as we walked down the hall. I don't normally feel threatened with this type of occasional touch, but something about the continual contact made me intensely uncomfortable.

A firm comment—"I'm not comfortable being touched"— or pulling away, showing discomfort, could both be acceptable ways of handling the problem. But then a risk presents itself: is it better to feel uncomfortable rather than creating disharmony and possibly damaging a new work relationship? While I didn't say anything to her, I think she sensed my discomfort, and that made our work relationship tense.

And remember that what you might think is an innocent touch could actually remind the recipient of a trauma from childhood or even in their current adult life. Abuse can leave scars that are hidden until they're triggered.

Your uncomfortable touch could uncork a raw emotion that could come out as anger, rage, or even a psychotic break. This is another reason to avoid intrusive physical contact at the workplace.

To be or not to be friendly

So what do you do about the space invader? You can try putting objects between you and the offender. Or gesture with your hands in a wide animated motion so the invader needs to back up.

While this might work from time to time, a frequent space invader might require a more direct message.

Another obvious, but difficult, tip might be to ask the invader not to touch you. Having this conversation right after an offensive act will help the offender acknowledge the problem. The degree to which you are firm, kind, and professional will determine if your work relationship thrives or wilts like yesterday's salad in the lunchroom fridge.

If an invader seems to require some sort of personal contact, offer a fist bump or a handshake. Make it obvious: that's as much contact as you want.

Getting a feel for what co-workers are comfortable with is part of building good working relationships. Watch how they act around others, and get a sense for what breaches their personal space. Some people are disturbed by having a co-worker just brush by them in a tight space. Others may not seem to mind a hand on the shoulder for an extended time or even a full-out hug.

Knowing the difference can help you dodge creating poor work vibes. When in doubt, follow the rule your kindergarten teacher taught you: keep your hands to yourself.

Expand your awareness

If a certain person continues to invade, and you know it isn't done maliciously, then try expanding your area of acceptance. Sometimes showing more love and acceptance in the workplace, in a very neutral way, can lead to a deeper work relationship. If you're more open, you might even feel encouraged and appreciated, too.

When we close ourselves off, co-workers are more likely to ignore us or appear standoffish. Of course, the goal isn't to be the workplace love-hippie bestowing peace and goodwill on all. But opening up can change the work dynamic and we might find more care and support from those around us.

But even if you don't feel comfortable with any amount of touch, that is okay. Everyone has the right to define their own boundaries while respecting others' right to do the same. If you feel that your sense of unwanted touch seems misaligned, you might want to consider seeing a professional therapist or doctor to help unravel your emotions.

I'm told I'm an invader

After analyzing your last interaction with a co-worker, you realized your encounters felt a bit off, and you're sure it's not your breath. After speaking with the co-worker or spending some time thinking about it, you now understand that it has to do with your constant childish pokes on the shoulder. Blessings to you.

Someone cared to tell you, to your face, that you are making them feel uneasy. Or you've managed to dig deeply enough on your own and realized that you've caused a problem. That's good—it means your activity hasn't crossed into harassment (yet). As hard as it is to look at criticism, try to find the good in it: there probably are others who didn't care for your space-invading habits, but didn't have the heart to tell you about their complaint. Now is the time to reassess what this means, and consciously implement some new behaviors and habits that provide the needed space. You may find your work relationships flowering, instead of co-workers dodging you like someone with a hygiene problem.

Nobody wants to be seen as the alien invader to avoid. Being conscious of space parameters, and being clear with co-workers about what you require is an important part of a healthy work relationship. Doing so is a sign of respect to those you work with every day.

 THREE TIPS FOR STAVING OFF THE INVADER

1. When dealing with a space invader, put an object like a chair between you and the offender, and gesture in an animated way so the invader needs to back up.

2. Tell the offender that your space bubble is large, so they understand your discomfort with touching. Having this communication right after an offense will help the offender acknowledge the problem.

3. If you're the invader, assess what you specifically do to make others uncomfortable. Form a new habit to respect a co-worker's personal space.

\ | /

IT'S IRRITATING TO SHARE

A WORK SPACE WITH

A CO-WORKER WHO

DOESN'T LIKE THEIR JOB,

IS TIRED OF WHAT THEY

DO, OR HAS BEEN IN THE

SAME POSITION SINCE

THE DINOSAUR AGE.

/ | \

Chapter 10

SHOULD I GO OR SHOULD I STAY? (MAYBE BOTH)

E VERYONE HAS BAD DAYS AT WORK FROM TIME TO TIME; for some, it's every day. It's likely you have wanted to quit your job at some point, especially on one of those bad days. But complaining out loud day in and day out, or even threatening to quit, creates poor morale for everyone within earshot. Soon employees who didn't have any problems at work start to echo your words and mimic your behavior, and that poor attitude then wafts through the office like the smell of scorched coffee.

Research shows that at any given time in the United States, as many as a third of employees are hanging onto a job they hate. And unfortunately, many of them aren't planning to vacate anytime soon. Sure, they may fantasize about the lure of a new job, but, for whatever reason, they choose to "quit and stay."

A person who quits but stays on the job can be damaging. They no longer are an asset but a liability. Employees who are unsatisfied let their work slide, rarely spend extra time at work, participate in drama (or even create it), and become poor representatives for the company in the eyes of customers and vendors.

Usually it is difficult to make someone who is dissatisfied with their job turn the corner toward happiness. Although a pay raise, a department shift, or a promotion might do the trick for a while, sooner or later that old feeling of wanting to leave a job returns with a vengeance.

It's irritating to share a work space with a co-worker who doesn't like their job, is tired of what they do, or has been in the same position since the dinosaur age. Everyone suffers. Attitudes degenerate. Nerves run raw. And intimidation is high. Not a great combination for a successful business atmosphere. It's usually better when an employee who would rather move on does just that.

A co-worker I once sat next to was the ultimate quitter-stayer. She'd begin on Monday morning, telling clients, "Only four more days left until Friday." Then she'd count down the hours until the end of the day. Soon making it to 5 o'clock on Friday was the only goal of the week. What message do you think clients and co-workers received? Another employee, when asked if he was having a good day, responded he wasn't happy until it was Friday. How do you think he performed Monday through Thursday? It was obvious these employees would rather have been anywhere but where they were sitting.

Playing that same broken record

When the economy is in a recession, fewer jobs are available. Employees can't move around as freely, so the feeling of being trapped can stifle any positive day-to-day experiences. On the other hand, when the economy is doing well, you might think a quitter-stayer would feel free to move on, but oddly many times that doesn't happen. Why?

Fear. That ugly word once again rears its head. It can paralyze a worker into staying by falsely declaring they aren't smart enough, and don't deserve happiness or more money. Fear can make someone feel more comfortable staying in a bad situation than moving on, simply because they've have been playing those same crappy recordings over and over in their minds and they haven't hit the stop button.

Possibly the thought of writing a resume, searching the employment listings, and putting themselves out there in a job interview is a scary process. Or, maybe there's fear related to self-image.

I worked with a man who seemed terribly unhappy at his job at times. I asked him why he didn't find a new, more enjoyable job. He replied he was too old and too heavy, his hair was too gray, and he dressed poorly, so no one would hire him. Why should he bother? His attitude became a self-fulfilling prophecy.

Other times, logistics such as a future cross-town commute can put the brakes on the search for a new job. Maybe the current job is near daycare or a fitness center, which makes it appealing to stay. Often, strange excuses surface that put the kibosh on beginning a job search: "I'm too tired after working all day" or "I'll never find a dentist I like close to my new work" or "The job I really want is second shift, but it's not a good move because I'll probably hit a deer coming home." I've actually heard these excuses! They are absurd when you look at them from a higher viewpoint.

And as workers get older, a move becomes more difficult. Not only do employees feel out of their comfort zone, but the learning curve takes longer when they're faced with new processes. So there's a wide range of reasons people stay at a hated job, foregoing what could be a shot at happiness.

Threatening to quit is a signal that something is wrong. A plea for help. While it would be nice if each worker took responsibility for their career and made changes when needed, sometimes employees feel stuck, unable to make a move. Whether it's their own limiting beliefs, the economy, or lack of direction, some people just can't seem to move on, either internally within the company or externally to a new job.

Not living the dream

Another reason workers quit and stay? They have a dream job in mind, but they also have lots of excuses as to why they can't quit to follow their inspiration. Instead of using their current job to enhance their skill set and their resume—learning new computer programs, studying lean manufacturing, or interfacing with new clients—they choose to put up a wall and look at the cement bricks.

Only that person can make the decision to change their work situation; you can't do it for them. If you hear them complaining, talk with them about what they want from a career. Maybe during your conversation, an idea will be planted about how they could rearrange their current work situation to align better with their desires.

I worked with a guy who enjoyed his job, but he really was not cut out for it. It required excellent recall and precision in details, which he lacked the skills to do appropriately. He ended up making many mistakes that cost the company money. He was well aware of his deficiencies, so he talked with his boss and decided to change jobs internally to something that suited him better. Once again he was able to enjoy this job.

Find a friend

Chatting over lunch or on break with a friend you trust can be a great stress reliever. Just talking about things going on in your life can be comforting and help you feel understood.

"Camaraderie is a key ingredient to happiness at work for male and female employees," says Christine Riordan, provost and professor of management at the University of Kentucky. She quotes a 2012 Gallup report that found that 50 percent of employees with a best friend at work reported feeling a strong connection with the company where they were employed, compared to 10 percent of employees without a best friend on the job.

Riordan adds, "Camaraderie is more than just having fun. It is also about creating a common sense of purpose and the mentality that we are in it together. Studies have shown that soldiers form strong bonds during missions in part because they believe in the purpose of the mission, rely on each other, and share the good and the bad as a team. In short, camaraderie promotes a group loyalty that results in a shared commitment to and discipline toward the work."

Infuse some passion

Those who express passion at work know the exhilaration of finding their proper lot in life and living it to the fullest. People with passion take fewer sick days, have more empathy for co-workers and client requests, and generally smile more.

What happens when you are forced to work with a group of less passionate co-workers? People who may be coasting in their jobs?

Frustration, to say the least.

It's not fun working with co-workers who do only the bare minimum, take the credit for everything, and never own up to mistakes. These type of people—let's call them coasters—actually strongly dislike passionate people. For coasters, passionate people threaten the status quo and remind them of their own deficiencies. An infusion of passion brings out the poor-me syndrome, and coasters find it as welcoming as poop in the pool.

Coasters can also intimidate new workers. I've seen people come to work at a new company only to find a manager or a co-worker continually calling out their mistakes or intentionally poking fun of them in front of other co-workers and managers. Why? The status quo has been upset, and the only way to get it back to the old level is to get rid of the new recruit.

This type of behavior causes a big problem for an employer, and, unfortunately, upper level management is rarely aware of it. Usually the offending coaster is one who's been around for many years who in the past has done a good job and is living on the shirt-tails of those memories.

If this behavior isn't nipped in the bud, new employees who can and should be bringing revitalizing blood into the workplace end up vacating the premises faster than a person who has just pulled the fire alarm.

Motivating Employees

How can organizations motivate employees so they feel engaged and stay with the company? Brent Peterson and Gaylan Nielson, authors of "How Do You Motivate Employees Who "Quit" But Stay," have outlined seven ways:

1. Explain the organization's goals and strategies to all employees.
2. Identify Real Work and the results the organization is seeking.
3. Share decision making with individuals and work teams.
4. Help employees align their work with their team.
5. Help employees and leaders adopt each other's perspectives.
6. Ensure that all learning is linked to organizational strategies.
7. Rethink Performance Management Processes (PMP).

Where's the beef?

Complainers really don't want to quit their job; otherwise they would have already done it. If you feel you can approach this subject with a co-worker, ask them what their biggest beef is. Is it the company in general? Is it management, lack of appreciation, a problem with a co-worker? Or you might learn that the person's home life is difficult, and that frustration is being transferred to the workplace. Sometimes people bring a whole suitcase of hidden issues with them to work. Taking time to talk about a problem and showing you care can sometimes defuse a situation and get productivity back on track.

I had a friend in the office who was in the process of getting a divorce. Usually a good worker, he had become testy and complained continuously about work and co-workers. When I talked with him over lunch, I found out his issues really had nothing to do with work. It had more to do with his unstable home life and it caused an imbalance in every other part of his life. He didn't know how to separate them, especially at work. Listening was the only thing I could offer him, and it seemed to help him through the rough time.

A temporary way station

At times, it may be you who has a feeling that something isn't right with your job. Don't discount those feelings. Those are exactly the feelings that will ultimately guide you to a happier work situation.

Maybe there are lots of good reasons to stay, for the time being. Look at your job as a way station, a temporary stop in life, and if you were completely prepared for a change, that change would have already happened. Perhaps you still have something to learn in your current environment so you can make a better, more informed decision. Or maybe you'll soon meet the right person who propels you in a new direction you hadn't considered.

My first job out of college was one that I enjoyed, but the company wasn't on the best footing with employees. Because of this tension, I wanted to leave my job, but being new to the industry, I wasn't sure where to go. One day production employees refused to come into work. Another business came in to help production continue to run until the matter was resolved. As a liaison for my employer, I worked with the outside company, and I realized how professional and enjoyable they were to work with. I asked them for a job, and they immediately said yes. My whole life changed with that single decision.

Other times, changing departments can offer the same results. Look for opportunities that fit, but at the same time, don't discount options that appear far-fetched. Those opportunities could be the ones that launch you into a brand-new arena and infuse passion into your day.

You are the artist, and passion is your paintbrush.

Often reminding yourself of the worthwhile elements of a job can be enough for gratitude to set in. It's amazing what happens when focus is redirected to the positive elements of a job rather than the negative. Try picking up a motivating book from the library or mediating to help gain a broader perspective. If you can't muster anything to be grateful about, remember that you're alive and reasonably healthy, and your job facilitates some independence.

Finding work you're passionate about can take a great deal of hard work, believe it or not, and can feel like a full-time job. Luckily, there are many self-help books, videos, web material, conferences, life coaches, and so on that can be utilized; but all of those things aren't worth the salt on your potatoes if you don't put a little gusto into your search. No one can do it for you.

I can hear your ego laughing. It's whispering in your ear all sorts of excuses as to why you can't, won't, and will never find passion. It's saying you can't leave your job just because you don't have passion. That is ridiculous.

If it isn't feasible to change jobs, try finding one small thing to make you happy and passionate at work. Look for the small gold nugget in the mountain of dull rock. If you like to write, offer to pen an article for the company newsletter. If you like to bake, whip up a bunch of goodies—sugar always makes people happy. Maybe you're sick of sitting at your desk all day long, and helping someone in your department with a new project might inject a little passion into your day.

Ways to Find Your Passion

1. Consider what makes you lose track of time. When you're so fully immersed that you're barely aware of things like time passing or being hungry.
2. Remember what you liked doing as a kid. One business consultant suggests making a list of everything you remember enjoying as a child and seeing how you can incorporate those activities into your current career.
3. Rule out what you *don't* want to do.
4. Read biographies. Does anyone in particular resonate with you?
5. Find the intersection between your strengths, your passions, and available career paths. Consider drawing three circles: one with

activities you love, one with things you do well, and one with decently paying positions. The intersection of those three circles could help you find a solution to your quandary.

6. Ask for advice carefully. One strategy might be to find successful people in each career path you're considering and reach out to them. That way you aren't asking friends and family who want the best for you but aren't necessarily familiar with the jobs.

7. Don't be afraid of choosing the wrong path. The worst that could happen is that you'll figure out what you don't like about that career field which will bring you one step closer to finding work you truly love.

—Shana Lebowitz, "Seven Simple Ways to Find Work You're Really Passionate About"

If nothing else, try listening. Listen to your own broken records; listen to your co-worker's stream of unhappy thoughts. Sometimes just using someone as a sounding board lets a little steam out of the whistle and gets you back on track to a healthier work attitude.

If the complainer can't seem to get out of that mode, then helping them move onto another job might be the best course of action.

Another avenue might be to talk to management about what might improve your workplace practices. Depending on the company's culture, you could create a movement to change office politics for the good, which in turn could change your outlook on life and your career.

Crystal ball, what do you say?

Remember, management doesn't have a crystal ball. If you don't know what your ideal job environment is, how can you expect someone else to have an epiphany? Some managers are really good at helping passionless employees find their spark again. They find out what makes people tick, create appropriate incentives, and watch the changes unfold. Others aren't so good at it. But don't blame them. It's your job to find the match and strike it.

If your co-worker isn't ready to take that step to find their passion, don't be surprised if they're not exactly thrilled when you do. Sometimes you need to let co-workers dig in the sand until they're ready to make their own castle.

Either way, it takes courage to find a new job, or to stay at your current position and make it better. You create the world in which you want to live in, whether you know it or not. So create one that is worth living. Believe me when I say that people will notice. You will feel energized and co-workers will be attracted to you, on an unconscious level, to your higher vibration. Life will feel good again. Right again—or maybe for the first time ever. Once you experience that, you'll never want to go back.

And as for that colleague who can't step up to the plate, remind them that being a respected quitter is far more admirable than being a complaining stayer.

THREE TIPS FOR DEALING WITH A QUITTER-STAYER

1. Ask your co-worker what they dislike about their job. Help them brainstorm ideas that they could do to change the situation to make it better.

2. Help a co-worker see all the positives, rather than the negatives, in their current job. They may realize the job isn't that bad.

3. If you're the quitter-stayer, try to discover your passions: find a book or try meditation. Or figure out a way to change your current job so it's more in line with your passions.

THE END GOAL
DEVELOPING TENACITY, HUMOR, AND GRACE IN THE WORKPLACE

T HIS BOOK SHOWCASES ONLY A HANDFUL OF PROBLEMS encountered in the work day. You might have many more to add to the repertoire of bad behaviors: like hygiene issues, stealing co-workers' lunches, microwaving smelly food, inappropriate dress, and excessive cologne/perfume. The list of behaviors that could annoy us is endless!

By reading this book you've learned some helpful techniques for dealing with co-worker issues as they arise, before they become ingrained and make you want to quit your job. And perhaps you've identified some behaviors in yourself that aren't exactly shining examples, and you're ready to sand off the sharp edges.

It's easy to put on the rose-colored glasses and point out a co-worker's mistakes. It's not so easy, however, to zero in on our own faults, slips-ups, and unconscious behavior and bring them into the open for examination. All sorts of emotions show up when we attempt to do this: fear, anxiety, disgust, anger, resistance, and feeling unconnected or alone. Those are powerful emotions, so it's no wonder we try to bury our heads in the sand and pretend, at all costs, that we're not the problem. It might just be that the bad behavior we dislike in others is reflecting something within ourselves.

If we can be honest, and we have the means to first recognize and then deal with our behaviors, we make progress. That's why it's so important to have a toolbox full of techniques to manage problems as they arise: listening to that quiet inner voice for guidance, meditating or contemplating, reciting a mantra, engaging our intuition, and allowing compassion into the situation. All these ways help us to climb to a level where we're almost a third-party observer watching the ego as it diabolically works against us. After recognizing an error and then digging deeper to understand its causes, we can forgive ourselves as well as others.

No one is perfect. To be human means to learn and grow from mistakes and go on with life. Part of this growth is to learn empathy for co-workers and their situations. While it is not okay to be a doormat, sometimes understanding people and their hardships can ease the tensions. It's extraordinary when the knots of karma break up, and trust and acceptance are allowed to ease into a situation.

If you're on the receiving end of bad behavior, don't let yourself fall into that co-worker's poor habits. It's easy to think, *"Well they do it, so I can too."* That just perpetuates the problem. We are so much more than our poor habits. Expect more from yourself, and others, and things will likely turn around.

There comes a time to reflect on who you truly are and decide whether your behavior mirrors that image. If it doesn't, then you have a prime opportunity to look inside and change yourself. It might not happen overnight, but each time you choose silence over gossiping, allow your ego to quit running your life, actively listen rather than interrupting, and find passion in your job, you are becoming more conscious of your role in the workplace and even in the world. When you fully acknowledge that you can't change others, but you can change how you view and act in a situation, then you have made amazing progress.

Think in terms of what is put out into the universe coming back to us—sometimes called the Law of Attraction—and it might help instill a little rigor to add compassion, patience, and consideration into our day. We attract our reality, no question about it. At some level, the people we choose to work with are a reflection of ourselves. You might say, "Wait a minute here. I didn't ask to work with this difficult person." Yes, that might be true, but you took the job and stayed. At this point, it's your job to see the opportunity that lies before you: an opportunity for growth and being conscious of poor behavior. Being conscious means you know and understand bad behavior and its effects. You now are more apt to be positive and raise the bar on what is acceptable. Use your power and strength within, and use it wisely.

The world is not a game that is won nor lost; it is a set of experiences that offer us rich lessons. Some lessons are painful. Some are enjoyable. Some are there to propel us up the steep staircase leading to wisdom.

The next time you encounter a difficult person, try with all your might to silently thank that person for being a teacher, for showing you the wrong way to handle a situation. Now you know better. And now you're starting to have a little tenacity, humor, and grace in the workplace. So keep your chin up and don't quit yet!

BIBLIOGRAPHY

PREFACE

"Census of Fatal Occupational Injuries Summary, 2014." Bureau of Labor Statistics, US Department of Labor, September 17, 2015. www.bls.gov/news.release/cfoi.nr0.htm.

Hananel, Sam. "Workplace Bullying Emerging as Major Employment Liability Battleground." *Insurance Journal*, March 4, 2013. www .insurancejournal.com/news/national/2013/03/04/283420.htm.

Lindblad, Marilyn. "What Is Considered Workplace Harassment?" Demand Media, 2016. everydaylife.globalpost.com/considered -workplace-harassment-5529.html.

Namie, Gary. "2014 WBI U.S. Workplace Bullying Survey." Workplace Bullying Institute. 2014. workplacebullying.org/multi/pdf/WBI -2014-US-Survey.pdf.

Namie, Gary, and Ruth Namie. "Frequently Asked Questions." Workplace Bullying Institute. 2015. www.workplacebullying.org/faq.

Petrone, Paul. "Survey: Nearly 1 in 3 Employees Is Looking for a New Job." *LinkedIn Talent Blog,* June 24, 2015. business.linkedin.com/ talent-solutions/blog/2015/06/survey-nearly-1-in-3-employees -is-looking-for-a-new-job.

Rapaport, Lisa. "Workplace Bullying May Increase the Risk of Suicidal Thoughts." Workplace Bullying Institute. September 2015. www .workplacebullying.org/suicide-3/#more-17882.

CHAPTER 1

Beck, Julie. "Have You Heard? Gossip Is Actually Good and Useful."
    Atlantic, November 6, 2014. www.theatlantic.com/health/
    archive/2014/11/have-you-heard-gossip-is-actually-good-and
    -useful/382430.

CHAPTER 2

International Online Training Program on Intractable Conflicts.
    "Active Listening." Conflict Research Consortium, University of
    Colorado. 1998. www.colorado.edu/conflict/peace/treatment/
    activel.htm.
Pedersen, Traci. "Mindfulness Can Aid Focus, Employee Bonds." *Psych*
    Central, March 2016. psychcentral.com/news/2016/03/13/
    workplace-mindfulness-increases-focus-fosters-employee
    -bonds/100367.html.
Strauss, Susan, RN, EdD. Author interview. March 2016.
Tolle, Eckhart. *A New Earth: Awakening to Your Life's Purpose*. New
    York: Dutton/Penguin, 2005.
Wildmind: Buddhist Meditation. "What Is Mindfulness?" 2015. www
    .wildmind.org/applied/daily-life/what-is-mindfulness.

CHAPTER 3

Finkelstein, Marion Grobb. "Why People Interrupt (and What to Do
    About It)." *MarionSpeaks* (blog), August 2, 2011. www.marion
    speaks.com/_blog/Marions_Communication_Tips/post/WHY_
    PEOPLE_INTERRUPT.

Nour, David. "I'll Excuse You for Talking While I'm Interrupting." *Huffington Post*, June 3, 2014. www.huffingtonpost.com/david -nour/ill-excuse-you-for-talkin_b_5432814.html.

CHAPTER 4

Roddick, Ellen. *Writing That Means Business—How to Get Your Message Across Simply and Effectively*. Bloomington, IN: iUniverse, 2010.

Shipley, David, and Schwalbe, Will. "The Email That Can Land You in Jail." Chapter 6 in *Send: Why People Email So Badly and How to Do It Better*. New York: Knopf, 2007.

Tschabitscher, Heinz. "How Many Emails Are Sent Every Day?" *About Tech*, September 2, 2015. email.about.com/od/emailtrivia/f/ emails_per_day.htm.

CHAPTER 5

El Kharzazi, Romella Janene, Mxolisi Siwatu, and Dexter R. Brooks. "Retaliation: Making It Personal." *Federal Manager* (Summer 2015): 9–13. www.eeoc.gov/laws/types/retaliation_considerations.cfm.

Hananel, Sam. "Workplace Bullying Emerging as Major Employment Liability Battleground." *Insurance Journal*, March 4, 2013. www .insurancejournal.com/news/national/2013/03/04/283420.htm.

Lindblad, Marilyn. "What Is Considered Workplace Harassment?" *GlobalPost*. everydaylife.globalpost.com/considered-workplace -harassment-5529.html. Accessed March 28, 2016.

Morem, Sue. "Ask Sue." Career Know How: weekly Q&A column. www .careerknowhow.com/ask_sue/space.htm.

Smith, CM. "6 Ways Journaling Will Chang Your Life". *Lifestyle*, 2012.

http://www.lifehack.org/articles/communication/how-to-build
-a-journaling-habit-in-28-days.html.

US Department of Labor—Civil Rights Center: Internal Statutes &
Regulations. "What Do I Need to Know About. . . Work
place Harassment." 2011. www.dol.gov.oasam/programs/
crc/2011-workplace-harassment.htm.

US Equal Employment Opportunity Commission. "Facts About Retaliation." www.eeoc.gov/laws/types/facts-retal.cfm.

US Equal Employment Opportunity Commission. "Facts About Sexual
Harassment." www1.eeoc.gov/eeoc/publications/fs-sex.cfm.

Workplace Bullying Institute. "2014 WBI U.S. Workplace Bullying
Survey." 2014. workplacebullying.org/multi/pdf/2014
-Survey-Flyer-B.pdf.

CHAPTER 6

Jacobson, Jeff. Author interview. March 2016.

Polly, Jean. "Surfing the Internet." *Netmom*, March 2008. www
.netmom.com/about-net-mom/25-meet-net- mom/26
-surfing-the-internet.html.

Spector, Lincoln. "How Dangerous Is Web Surfing?" *PC World,* July 25,
2011. www.pcworld.com/article/231146/surf_warning.html.

CHAPTER 7

Estroff Marano, Hara. "Procrastination: Ten Things To Know: Is Your
Procrastination Hindering You?" *Psychology Today*, August
2003. www.psychologytoday.com/articles/200308/
procrastination-ten-things-know.

Mind Tools Editorial Team. "Overcoming Procrastination: Manage Your Time, Get It All Done." Mind Tools. www.mindtools.com/pages/article/newHTE_96.htm. Accessed March 21, 2016.

CHAPTER 8

Counter, Jim. Author interview. March 2016.

Skoglund, Linda. Author interview. March 2016.

Walters, Brad. "Hiring and Working with Family." *Business Week*, March 22, 2011. www.businessweek.com/smallbiz/tips/archives/2011/03/hiring_and_working_with_family.html.

CHAPTER 9

McQuerrey, Lisa. "Respecting a Co-Worker's Personal Space." *Global Post*. everydaylife.globalpost.com/respecting-coworkers -personal-space-9496.html. Accessed March 28, 2016.

CHAPTER 10

Gregoire, Carolyn. "Why You Should Care About Having Friends at Work." *Huffington Post*, July 17, 2013. www.huffingtonpost .com/2013/07/08/work-relationships_n_3561568.html.

Lebowitz, Shana. "Seven Simple Ways to Find Work You're Really Passionate About." *Business Insider*, June 1, 2015. www.business insider.com/how-to-find-work-youre-passionate-about-2015-6.

Peterson, Brent D., and Gaylan Nielson. "How Do You Motivate Employees Who 'Quit' But Stay?" TLNT: Talent Management and

HR. *Ere Media*, December 1, 2010. www.eremedia.com/tlnt/how
-do-you-motivate-employees-who-quit-but-stay/.

Petrone, Paul. "Survey: Nearly 1 in 3 Employees Is Looking for a New
Job." Talent Trends 2015 Report. *LinkedIn Talent Blog*, June 24,
2015. business.linkedin.com/talent-solutions/blog/2015/06/
survey-nearly-1-in-3-employees-is-looking-for-a-new-job.

RECOMMENDED READING

Acuff, Jon. *Quitter: Closing the Gap Between Your Day Job and Your Dream Job*. Brentwood, TN: Lampo, 2011.

Crowley, Katherine, and Kathi Elster. *Mean Girls at Work: How to Stay Professional When Things Get Personal*. New York: McGraw-Hill, 2013.

Kabat-Zinn, Jon. *Mindfulness for Beginners: Reclaiming the Present Moment—and Your Life*. Boulder, CO: Sounds True, 2012.

Roddick, Ellen. *Writing That Means Business: How To Get Your Message Across Simply and Effectively*. Bloomington, IN: iUniverse, 2010.

Shimoff, Marci. *Happy for No Reason: 7 Steps to Being Happy from the Inside Out*. New York: Free Press, 2008.

Shipley, David, and Schwalbe, Will. *Send: Why People Email So Badly and How to Do It Better*. New York: Knopf, 2007.

Tolle, Eckhart. *A New Earth: Awakening to Your Life's Purpose*. New York: Dutton/Penguin, 2005.

WORKBOOK

Part 1

Answer the following questions by yourself in a quiet space.

1. List all the current conflicts you are experiencing with co-workers (include managers and bosses if you want).

2. Describe how you feel about these conflicts. Be specific. (Do you feel annoyed, angry, fearful that you'll lose your job?)

3. As you see it, how do these conflicts affect other employees?

4. Have you ever tried to tell someone their workplace behavior isn't appropriate? If so, what was the outcome?

5. What could you as an individual employee do to make your place of work a more positive environment?

6. What could you do to lessen the impact of these conflicts on your work life? Examples: take a class, learn to meditate, find a mantra that guides you through an incident. Think outside the box.

Part 2

These exercises can be used as either a team-building activity or tools for mediating a conflict between two or more co-workers.

For a team-building activity, form a group. Choose co-workers who work closely together. Appoint a circle leader to lead the exercises. This person should not be a manager, boss, or human resources representative, so that all employees involved are peers. Someone outside the department or even the company would be the best choice for circle leader to ensure that conversations don't get bogged down in accusations or interpersonal conflicts.

If this exercise is being used as a tool for mediating a conflict between two or more co-workers, a manager or HR representative should officiate the meeting.

The leader's job is to talk to HR or management *before* the team-building or conflict resolution meeting and make a list of top problems they see affecting employees. By doing this ahead of time, emotion is taken out of the problem, making it less personal, so that employees are more apt to begin a dialogue. Also, communicate clearly to employees before they begin the activity that the reason for these exercises is *not* to point fingers, but ultimately to create more respect for each other, decrease work disruptions, and make the team more productive.

Exercise 1

Form a circle. Have each person start by describing one conflict on the leader's list and talk about why and how it affects them. Remind participants not to refer to specific employees. Have someone write down each complaint on a whiteboard or a large piece of paper so everyone can refer back to it; you'll need it for the next exercise.

Exercise 2

Form small groups of two or three people. Have each group take one of the conflicts from the list and role-play a scenario about it in front of the entire group. (Again, names of actual employees should not be used.) After each role-play, have everyone try to articulate how each person felt in the scenario and what effects the conflict had on the workplace. Participants can write down their thoughts and then offer them in group discussion.

Exercise 3

Have the small groups go back and role-play the same conflict, but show what a more positive outcome looks like. Think in terms of what respect looks and sounds like.

Exercise 4

As a large group, have employees write down how they think they could change their own behavior to help make the work environment more positive.

Exercise 5

Sometimes improvements are made immediately after a discussion, but they may not last. So encourage participants to think ahead: talk about what management could do to make this a lasting change so behavior can't revert back to the old ways. Again, everyone should attempt to think outside the box, and not only of appropriate reprimands, but also about how positive actions could be rewarded.

Exercise 6

Have each member say one thing they appreciate about the person to their right. It could be one word or a sentence. Sometimes this is tough, especially if not everyone gets along. But it could be something as simple as mentioning the cookies they share with co-workers or the fact that they are on time for meetings. This exercise is designed to discover respect and common ground even when frustration has set in.

NOTES

ACKNOWLEDGMENTS

I'd like to thank all the "teachers" I have worked with: people who have taught me the greatest lessons on earth about what it means to be a co-worker who treats others with respect. At the time, I wasn't so thrilled to have these lessons thrust upon me, but looking back I can see how much I have grown. These lessons have made me a better co-worker, wife, mother, and friend.

I'd also like to thank my editor, Beth Wright, for her willingness to offer me the truth no matter what, never sugarcoating the facts. She always nudged me to write from my heart in a way that speaks to others in the clearest way possible. She has helped me realize how important my words are for those who are facing challenges at work and have no idea how to handle them.

Next, I'd like to offer a sincere note of thanks to my daughter, Ashley, for allowing me to bounce ideas off her for weeks on end, sometimes even in the dead of the night when I had a sudden epiphany. She was also instrumental in the layout of this book. Ashley, I know someday you will do something remarkable and worthy because you are a kind and generous person who touches the hearts of others.

Lastly, I'd like to thank the friends who read my book many times before it was published and provided suggestions, comments, and advice. I am constantly amazed at the great friendships I have in my life and how blessed I truly am.

ABOUT THE AUTHOR

Debbra Anne is dedicated to helping workers soar high with their mindful actions, teamwork, and healthy work relationships. Debbra's passion has spurred companies to reevaluate what is poor, nonproductive behavior and help employees change their own thinking to improve workplace culture.

Debbra is also the author of *The Enlightened Cat: 12 Feline Lessons in Life and Spirituality*. Her love of cats, along with a deep love of spiritual principles, has helped readers realize the importance of animals and the lessons we can learn from them. A portion of the proceeds from that book goes to an animal shelter near Debbra's home in western Wisconsin.

Website: www.DebbraAnne.com
Twitter: Debbra_Anne
Facebook: www.facebook.com/DebbraAnne/